Dear Fr...

I'd like to take this opportunity to personally thank you for visiting one of our many offices to pick up this cook book. May it provide you, your family and friends many hours of pleasant dining.

We hope this book will always remind you that there is ALWAYS something "cooking" at American Savings. We can provide you with the highest quality ingredients available to anyone, including:

★ **SAFETY SINCE 1885**

★ **CAPITAL AND RESERVES <u>OVER TWICE</u> LEGAL REQUIREMENTS**

★ **ASSETS OVER 4¼ <u>BILLION</u> DOLLARS STRONG**

★ **NATION'S <u>HIGHEST INTEREST</u> ON INSURED SAVINGS**

★ **MANY FREE SERVICES WITH SPECIFIED MINIMUM BALANCES**

★ **CONVENIENT LOCATIONS**

★ **PLEASANT AND HELPFUL COUNSELORS TO SERVE YOU**

We know you will find these ingredients to your liking, and that is why American Savings is one of the NATION'S LARGEST financial institutions.

Remember, at American Savings YOU *NEVER* LOSE, YOU *ALWAYS GAIN!* And, Bon Appétit!

Sincerely,

S. Mark Taper

S. Mark Taper, Chairman of the Board

AMERICAN SAVINGS AND LOAN ASSOCIATION

The International Chafing Dish Cook Book

Leonard Louis Levinson

BANTAM BOOKS
TORONTO · NEW YORK · LONDON

For Stanley and Sylvia

THE INTERNATIONAL CHAFING DISH COOK BOOK
A Bantam Book / published July 1971
2nd printing
3rd printing

Published simultaneously in the United States and Canada

Bantam Books are published by Bantam Books, Inc., a National
General company. Its trade-mark, consisting of the words "Bantam
Books" and the portrayal of a bantam, is registered in the United
States Patent Office and in other countries. Marca Registrada.
Bantam Books, Inc., 666 Fifth Avenue, New York, N.Y. 10019.

PRINTED IN THE UNITED STATES OF AMERICA

Acknowledgments

"RECEIVED WITH THANKS"

The above is the cheery and polite way British shopkeepers receipt their bills. And it is the phrase I wish to use in acknowledging, with gratitude, the many recipes I have been given to include in this book. There are so many people, I am going to list them alphabetically. Thank you—

Capt. Scarritt Adams, U.S.N. Ret., of Bermuda; Phil Alpert, Cheeses of all Nations, N.Y.C.; Teress Altschul, Los Angeles, Calif.; Armando Armanni, Hotel Excelsior, Rome.

Rainer F. Baldauf, Señor Pico Restaurant, San Francisco, Calif.; Pierre Barrelet, Gritti Palace Hotel, Venice; Walter Baxter, The Chanterelle, London; Fred and Neill Beck, Westlake Village, Calif.; Peter S. Bugoni and staff, Baroque Restaurant, N.Y.C.

Comm. Giorgio Campione, director general of the C.I.G.A. hotels of Italy; Rosemary Cartwright of Washington, D.C.; Constance Carr of Bangor, Maine; Bruno Carvaggi of Quo Vadis Restaurant, N.Y.C.; Mr. Chacham, Cheese Unlimited, N.Y.C.; H. R. Cornwell, English Country Cheese Council, London; John Philips Cranwell, Washington, D.C.

Bruno M. Dedual, The Peninsula Hotel, Hong Kong; Marina Deserti, Bologna, Italy.

Konrad Egli, Chalet Suisse, N.Y.C.; Felice Earley, N.Y.C.

Anita Fiel, American Spice Trade Assn., N.Y.C.; Julian Freirich Co., Long Island City, N.Y.

Mrs. Doris Gospe, Santa Rosa, Calif.; Vivian Gronback, Heublein, Inc., Hartford, Conn.

John Milton Hagen, Mill Valley, Calif.; Marcia Hale, Zurich, Switzerland; Johnny Hines and Bill Smart, East Boston, Mass.; J. D'Hoir, Hotel Meurice, Paris; E. Roxie Howlett, Diamond Walnut Kitchen, San Francisco, Calif.; Cathi Hunt, The Underwood Kitchens, Boston, Mass.; Marjorie Child Husted, Minneapolis, Minn.

Gordon Irving, Glasgow, Scotland; Herb Isaacson, Cheese Village, Ltd. and La Fondue, N.Y.C.

Paul Jacob, The Monk's Inn, N.Y.C.; Vernon Jarratt, George's Restaurant, Rome; Daryl Jason, N.Y.C.; Julius, Maître d'Hôtel, Luchow's Restaurant, N.Y.C.

Grace Teed Kent, Longchamps Restaurants, N.Y.C.; Mimi Kilgore, Tiburon, Calif.; Joe Ann Kilian, Palos Verde Peninsula, Calif.; Olga v. Kollar of Sorella Fontana, Rome and Bologna.

René Lasserre, Lasserre Restaurant, Paris; Mary Lehrbaummer, Oster, Milwaukee, Wisconsin; Claude Lemercier, Hotel de Crillon, Paris; Traudi Lessing, Vienna; Joyce Levinson, West Los Angeles, Calif.; Robert M. Levinson, La Cañada, Calif.; Sidnee Livingston, N.Y.C.; Paola Lucentini, N.Y.C.

Loys C. Malmgren, General Foods Kitchens, White Plains, N.Y.; Hester Marsden-Smedley, London; Matsushita Electric Corp. of America, N.Y.C.; Arnaldo Meo, Danieli Royal Excelsior Hotel, Venice; M. Miconi, Excelsior Grand Hotel Principi di Piemonte-Torino; Faith and MacGowan Miller, N.Y.C.; Gloria Mohr, San Jose, Calif.; John R. Moot, Cornwall Corp., Boston; Charles Morgenstern, Freeport, L.I., N.Y.; LaMar Mulliner, N.Y.C.; Mary Murphy, Borden, Inc., N.Y.C.

National Presto Industries, Inc., Eau Claire, Wisc.

Shirley O'Neill, Hunt-Wesson Kitchens, Fullerton, Calif.

Miss Gene Poll, The Sterno Co., New York City.

Maurice Renault, Agent Littéraire, Paris; Massimo Rosati, Hotel Excelsior, Naples; Florence Rypinski, Honolulu, Hawaii.

Mimi (Mrs. Tony) Sandler, Ogilvie, Minn.; V. Schachner, Palace Hotel, Milan; Lucille Schulberg, N.Y.C.; Alice Scully, Palm Springs, Calif.; Evalyn Santiago, Solana Beach, Calif.; Bernard Simon, N.Y.C.; Maryellen Spencer, Dudley-Anderson-Yutzy, N.Y.C.; Alice Stanley, Santa

Monica, Calif.; Muriel Stevens, Channel Five, Las Vegas, Nev.

Ch. Teichmann, Fouquet's Restaurant, Paris; Roger Topolinski, Restaurant Lapérouse, Paris.

Joy and Jo Van Ronkel, Beverly Hills, Calif.; Jacques Valentin, Deauville, France.

Reah Wachsman of West Los Angeles, Calif.; Charlotte Westberg, Lausanne, Switzerland; Mary Lee Gray Westcoat, Uniontown, Pa.; Arthur S. Wenzel, La Fonda Restaurant, Los Angeles, Calif., and last, but far from least, Sonia Wolfson, Beverly Hills, Calif.

Once more, I thank you from the bottom of my page.

THE AUTHOR

Contents

Introduction

CHAFING DISHERY

The word "chafing" comes from the French *chauffer,* meaning to heat or warm. The original *chauffeurs* were firemen on steam cars.

Chafing dish cookery was probably first introduced into elegant homes by chefs from the top Paris restaurants in the 1800's and from there it spread across the English Channel (which the French modestly call "The Sleeve") to posh British homes in the Victorian era. Every fair damsel was expected to woo her favorite beau by dishing up some speciality in her chafing dish. On the other hand, the wicked bachelor of the times lured his inamorata to his flat for a cozy supper for two highlighted by a hot concoction he concocted himself on his table-top cooking equipment. One daring chef-seducer wrote a cookbook with each item named after a fair victim who supposedly yielded under the blandishment of one of his recipes, such as "Lady Effingham's Eggs" and "Duchess of Cambridge's Frog Legs."

Which reminds me of the autograph I once wrote in a copy of my *Brown Derby Cookbook:* "To _____, the one dish I wish I knew how to make."

However, the chafing dish, or some likely counterpart, goes far back beyond the Victorian age. Something similar can be seen at the Metropolitan Museum of Art in New York City among the effects of Egyptian pharaohs; they have been unearthed at Pompeii and Herculaneum, whether used for heating or cooking is not known; and they were utilized both at the dinner table and in camp, with charcoal as fuel, from the Middle Ages on.

Long a utensil wielded by upper-crust amateurs (as well as upper-crust restaurant captains and waiters), in

1

very recent times the chafing dish has spread through all social strata (which are becoming less distinguishable all the time). And with that popularity has come a much wider use of the equipment, escalating from simple Welsh Rabbits to almost every kind of dish: appetizers, soups, pastas, other cheese concoctions, fish, meat and main dishes, beverages and, especially, desserts.

Along with these adaptations from other forms of cooking have also come newly-created dishes, as, for example, the dozen different other national versions of Welsh Rabbit which I have invented for this book.

ENTERTAINING IN A CHAFING DISH

This calls for your sharpest showmanship skills. Rehearse what you are going to do, even if only in your mind. Have everything you need within handy reach, including those foods which must be cooked in advance. Follow each step carefully, if blithely.

Use your finest silver and linens, being careful to protect table and linen from heat by using trays, etc., under the chafing dish. Or, use any old silver, plus expendable or disposable tablecloths and napkins, all depending upon the company invited.

Even if you don't use your chafing dish to concoct recipes at the table, use it to keep food warm and for having buffet items at a pleasing temperature. The appeal of a chafing dish is not only to the eye, but to the smell as well as the palate.

Perfect your skills with the chafing dish and you will add another dimension to your personality—and your reputation.

TO BE SPECIFIC

Have everything you need ready beforehand, either on table or alongside on a service or tea cart. Arrange ingredients and utensils attractively, in the order of their use. Your accessories should be good conversation pieces.

A wooden spoon or rubber spatula makes a good stirrer

which is noiseless and doesn't interfere with conversation—for you will be expected to talk or lead the talk while you perform.

Have sliced, diced, grated foods ready in the form called for in the recipe; mix seasonings beforehand; have ingredients at room temperature, unless otherwise specified.

Be skillful at flaming a dish as the climax of its preparation, using liquors, liqueurs or wines of high alcoholic content. Both the liquor and the food to be flamed should be heated, though not boiling. Pour heated liqueur over food and then ignite. Do not ignite while pouring unless you've invited your friendly neighborhood fire chief.

Long fireplace matches or tapers are ideal to use. Or tip the edge of the blazer pan so that fumes from the warm liqueur at the edge of pan are ignited by flame of heat source.

Use long-handled spoon or ladle and keep basting flames until they die out and only the flavor and aroma of the liqueur remains. See more about Flaming further on.

THE CHAFING DISH

The chafing dish consists of 4 components:

1. A cover, with knob, that fits over the blazer pan (or the water pan).

2. The blazer pan, with handle, is the part you use the most. It serves for cooking everything, either over direct heat or over a water bath which functions like the lower half of a double boiler.

3. The water pan or bath or well which fits over the heating base and under the blazer pan. Used to provide an even heat below the boiling point. Add *hot* water if more is needed.

4. The heating base, which contains the alcohol or Sterno fuel container or the butane or electric heating element. In the latter case, there are heat controls with dial, divided into temperature ranges.

Never heat *empty* chafing dish pans, as this can cause warping and injure the finish.

Almost any recipe made in a skillet or frying pan can be executed at the table in a chafing dish—if it does not require too much time, too much heat or cause air pollution.

Pancakes, fritters, toasted sandwiches, and every variation of scrambled eggs, as well as thin steaks, pasta sauces, grilled vegetables and dessert crêpes are among the dishes that can be whipped up in a deft, showmanly manner in your chafing dish.

And, using the water pan under the blazer pan, you can enlarge your repertoire to include any dishes which must be heated carefully at lower than frying temperatures—or those prepared beforehand but kept at exactly the right warmed heat while eating . . . and for seconds.

BUYING YOUR CHAFING DISH

One of the best ways of acquiring a chafing dish is to receive it as a present, which is the way a lot of people first get them. If you have one that has been gathering dust on an upper shelf, this book should eliminate any excuse you might have had for not using it.

But if you are going out to buy a chafing dish, shop around, ask friends who have them what they consider the best kind to buy. Have the salesman at the store show you all the components and how they work. Be sure you get the available literature which comes with the appliance you buy.

If it is a butane c.d. be sure you know how it works and how it is fueled. And if it is one of the electric ones, be sure that it has the Underwriters Laboratory stamp of approval and that you have the proper current, voltage, and wattage in your house.

Lastly, make sure the capacity of the chafing dish you purchase fits your entertainment plans.

A Catalog of Chafing Dish Equipment is at the end of the book.

A FEW SIMPLE RULES FOR CHAFING DISH COOKERY

Unless your guests like to linger long over drinks at the table, use recipes that don't take long to cook in front of the company. Longer-cooking ones can be partially cooked beforehand.

Arrange ingredients in advance, either on the table or a service cart alongside, so they are at your fingertips and in the proper order.

Either memorize the recipe, or have brief notes of the steps on a small card on the tray. After the second time, you won't need this prompting.

Keep the lights low.

Keep the guest list small.

Keep the food simple but elegant.

FLAMING WARNING!

Although you may have seen a maître d' or captain of waiters pouring brandy or liqueur directly from the bottle onto a flaming dish, *do not try it*.

Always heat the alcoholic addition in a flameproof pot, then pour on the pan or dish and ignite, making sure the chemical fumes of the match have burned away first.

This is always a somewhat spectacular sight. (I remember a French restaurant in San Marino, California, where the lights were lowered and a recording of "Ave Maria" permeated the atmosphere.) But the actual purpose of this culinary hotfoot is to burn off the alcohol, leaving the flavor of the liquor.

Ah, if the Russian circus producers would only train one of their intelligent bruins to play maître d' with a flaming chafing dish, put a Boy Scout hat on his head, and serve Crêpes à la Smoky the Bear, what an act they'd have!

Chafing Dish Appetizers

The chafing dish is a handy help to the hostess who seeks to serve her guests hot hors d'oeuvre at a cocktail party, buffet or simply as preliminary to dinner.

It enables her to prepare the dish in advance, if she cares to, and have it simmer, kept at the most appetizing temperature in the blazer pan over a hot water bath for the duration of the party, needing no attention—except, maybe, to pour in refills due to the depredations of the delighted eaters. Thus, the lady of the house can be a guest at her own party.

Here are a score of recipes for a variety of chafing dishes, any of which will make a hit, either by itself or with the addition of a few cold hors d'oeuvre.

P.S. Almost all of them will also serve as main dishes, feeding from 4 to 6 people. And, on the other hand, almost any other chafing dish recipe in this book can be used as a cocktail-time attraction.

CANAPE MARGUERY
[Serves 2]

1 green pepper, seeded and trimmed
1 sweet red pepper, seeded and trimmed
1 3½-ounce can tuna, drained
6 anchovy filets
1 large hard-cooked egg
Butter
Russian dressing

Chop peppers, tuna, anchovies and egg. Sauté in butter in blazer pan until hot. Add enough Russian dressing to moisten well. Heat again. Serve over thick buttered, trimmed toast.

7

HOT COCKTAIL BITS
[Serves 24]

1 pound bologna, cut in cubes	1 pound cocktail sausages
1 pound salami, cut in cubes	Melted butter
1 pound frankfurters, in slices	Toothpicks
Dipping sauces	

Preheat blazer pan over medium flame.

Dip cubes, slices and sausages in butter and grill until brown on all sides. Remove by spearing with toothpicks and serve on warm plates covered with paper doilies or napkins.

Mustard, relish, pickle and hot dog sauces can be used for dipping.

CHEESED HOT DOGS
[Makes about 60]

1 cup dry white wine	1 teaspoon Worcestershire sauce
1½ cups Cheddar cheese in cubes	½ teaspoon dry mustard
½ cup Swiss cheese in cubes	4 5-ounce packages cocktail sausages or wieners
1 tablespoon cornstarch	
Dash Tabasco sauce	

Heat wine in blazer pan of electric chafing dish at high until bubbles begin to rise to the surface.

Put cheeses, cornstarch, Worcestershire, mustard and Tabasco into container of blender, add heated wine, cover and blend at high until smooth.

Pour into blazer pan and place over hot water at high, stirring constantly until smooth and thickened. Reduce heat to medium; add sausages and heat through.

Spear wieners or sausages with cocktail picks or skewers and serve with rounds of party rye bread or crackers.

Neill and Fred Beck, who wrote the memorable *Farmer's Market Cook Book,* have given me this recipe which can either be served in a chafing dish as an hors d'oeuvre or with rice as a supper dish.

BABY MEAT BALLS
[Serves 12 as appetizer, 4 as main dish]

4 tablespoons olive oil
1 medium onion, chopped fine
1 clove garlic, pierced by toothpick
4 large mushroom caps, chopped fine

⅔ cup red wine
1 teaspoon Worcestershire sauce
1 pound ground steak
⅓ cup hot water
Salt and pepper
1 teaspoon chopped parsley
1 teaspoon chopped chives

Heat 2 tablespoons of the olive oil in a saucepan; add chopped onion and garlic clove and brown them. Add mushrooms and cook together 2 minutes. Add ⅓ cup of the red wine and Worcestershire; heat but do not boil. Remove mixture from fire and discard garlic. Allow to cool.

In a bowl blend the mixture with the ground round, mixing thoroughly, but with a light touch. Form into balls 1 inch or less in diameter.

Heat remaining 2 tablespoons olive oil in pan and brown meat balls. When evenly browned and cooked, transfer meat balls to blazer pan of chafing dish.

Pour off extra fat from pan that cooked meat balls, add remaining ⅓ cup of red wine and ⅓ cup hot water. Simmer and scrape bottom of pan until all the brown residue sticking to pan has been absorbed by liquid. Add salt and pepper to taste and parsley and chives. Pour over meat balls in blazer pan, keeping all warm with medium flame. Serve with cocktail picks.

SPICY COCKTAIL MEAT BALLS
[Makes about 60]

1 4¾-ounce can liverwurst spread
¾ pound lean ground beef
1 teaspoon prepared mustard
1½ teaspoons salt

⅛ teaspoon pepper
½ cup packaged fine dry breadcrumbs
1 egg, slightly beaten
¾ cup finely crushed corn chips
Chili sauce

Combine liverwurst, beef, and seasonings until well-blended. Add breadcrumbs and egg, mix thoroughly. Form into 1-inch balls using a rounded teaspoonful. Roll balls in crushed corn chips. Broil on a rack 6 inches from heat for 4 to 5 minutes; turn balls and broil another 4 to 5 minutes. Serve warm in chafing dish, with chili sauce.

Balls may be covered tightly and refrigerated overnight. Just before broiling, roll in crushed corn chips.

Here is an appetizer recipe from the celebrated Hotel Fontainebleau in Miami Beach.

BEEF AND WALNUT BALLS BAVARIAN
[Makes about 50]

1 pound ground round beef	½ teaspoon seasoned pepper
2 eggs, beaten	Peanut oil for frying
1 cup fine-chopped walnuts	½ cup Madeira wine
1 teaspoon garlic salt	½ cup undiluted consommé
1 teaspoon seasoned salt	2 tablespoons tomato paste

Combine beef, eggs, walnuts, salts and pepper until well mixed. Shape into small balls about ¾ inch in diameter. Sauté quickly in heated oil in blazer pan until they brown lightly. Drain off fat. Add wine to pan, heat; ignite and shake pan gently until flames die out. Blend in consommé and tomato paste. Simmer over low heat until meat balls are tender, about 5 to 10 minutes.

And here is a chafing dish appetizer from the kitchen of Jim Beard, courtesy of the Sterno people.

SHRIMP CASANOVA
[Serves 4]

1 pound shrimp
4 tablespoons butter
4 thin slices French bread
3 tablespoons minced onion
1 teaspoon shredded carrot
1 teaspoon dried tarragon
   leaf
  Salt and fresh-ground
   pepper

½ cup dry white wine or
  vermouth
¼ cup cognac or vodka
  (optional)
Toasted bread slices
Lemon slices
Chopped parsley

Shell and devein shrimp; or use frozen prepared shrimp, thawed. Keep in refrigerator until ready to use.

Melt half of butter in blazer pan or crêpe pan of chafing dish over direct flame. Add French bread and toast lightly on both sides. Remove to warm plate.

Add remainder of butter and cook onion until yellow, stirring occasionally. Add shrimp and carrot; sprinkle with tarragon, salt and pepper to taste. Sauté 4 minutes, then add wine and bring to a slow simmer. Shrimp should be pink and just about done. To flame, remove pan from heat and pour heated cognac or vodka over shrimp. Ignite. When flame dies, arrange toasted bread slices and lemon slices around pan. Sprinkle with chopped parsley.

Out in Santa Rosa, California, fresh crab are usually available. That is what Doris Gospe uses. If you are not in a fresh crab area, substitute 1 can of crabmeat.

FRESH CRAB CANAPE
[Makes 2 cups]

1 good-sized fresh crab
Juice of 1 lemon
1 8-ounce package cream cheese
¼ cup heavy cream
¼ cup mayonnaise
1 teaspoon minced onion
½ teaspoon minced chives
½ clove garlic, crushed
Sprinkle Worcestershire sauce
Pinch salt
2 drops Tabasco sauce

Remove meat from crab and marinate in lemon juice at least 1 hour.

Whip together cream cheese, cream, mayonnaise, onion, chives, garlic, Worcestershire, salt and Tabasco until smooth. Fold in crabmeat.

Warm in chafing dish and serve with wheat crackers.

MARY LOU MORGAN'S CRAB DIP
[Makes 2 cups]

1 8-ounce package cream cheese, creamed with 1 tablespoon cream
6½ ounces flaked crab
(canned, frozen or fresh)
2 tablespoons minced onion
½ teaspoon horseradish
¼ teaspoon salt

Mix all ingredients together, transfer to baking dish and bake in 375° oven 25 minutes.

Turn out into chafing dish and serve as a dip with a firm chip, such as Fritos or crinkle-cut potato chips.

From Mrs. Sidnee Livingston, the painter, when she entertains in her Greenwich Village studio, comes this

CURRIED VEGETABLE DIP
[Makes about 4 cups]

1/3 cup chopped onions	2 cups milk
1/3 cup butter	1/2 cup moist shredded
2 tablespoons flour	coconut
2 1/2 tablespoons curry powder	1/2 cup plumped raisins
1 1/2 teaspoons salt	Squeeze lemon juice
1 teaspoon sugar	1/2 cup cream
4 whole cloves	
Pinch cayenne pepper	

In blazer pan of chafing dish, sauté the onions in melted butter. When onions are transparent, blend in flour and cook until bubbling. Add curry powder, salt, sugar, cloves and cayenne. Mix well.

Remove from heat and gradually stir in milk.

Return to heat and stir until sauce thickens, about 15 minutes. Add coconut and raisins and cook a few minutes more. Add lemon juice and keep stirring. Gradually add the cream and blend well. Serve with carrot, celery, cucumber sticks, cauliflowerets, etc.

Variation: An excellent Curried Shrimp can be made by following above recipe and adding 1 pound cooked shrimp after the cream and cooking until sauce and shrimp are thoroughly heated.

SWISS DIP
[Makes 2 cups]

1/2 pound grated Swiss cheese	1/4 cup catsup
1 4 1/2-ounce can deviled ham	1/4 cup Bourbon (optional)

Melt cheese in blazer pan over hot water. Add deviled ham, catsup, and Bourbon. Serve hot with assorted dippers and crackers, preferably unsalted.

HIGH-LIFE LIVERS
[Serves 12]

2 pounds chicken livers
1 teaspoon salt
Flour
4 tablespoons butter or
    margarine
1/2 teaspoon dried oregano
1 teaspoon Worcestershire

sauce
2 teaspoons parsley flakes
1/4 teaspoon powdered thyme
1/4 pound mushrooms, sliced
1 tablespoon lemon juice
2 tablespoons sherry
    (optional)

Sprinkle chicken livers with salt and dredge in flour; set aside.

Melt butter in blazer pan of 2-quart chafing dish. Add oregano, Worcestershire sauce, parsley flakes and thyme; mix well.

Sauté half the chicken livers for 10 to 15 minutes, stirring occasionally. Remove from pan and sauté remaining half of livers with mushrooms, adding more butter if needed.

Return cooked livers to pan; sprinkle lemon juice and sherry over. Heat thoroughly. Serve on English muffins or toast.

ANGELS ON HORSEBACK
[Makes about 30]

30 fresh or 1 12-ounce can
    oysters
2 tablespoons chopped
    parsley
1/2 teaspoon salt

Paprika
Fresh-ground pepper
10 slices bacon, cut in thirds
Hot buttered toast sections
    (optional)

If frozen oysters are used, thaw them. Drain oysters; sprinkle with parsley and seasonings. Place an oyster on each 1/3 piece of bacon, wrap bacon around oyster and fasten with a toothpick.

Place them in blazer pan and fry until bacon is crisp on one side. Turn and fry other side until crisp. Serve as is or on pieces of hot buttered toast.

Imported from the islands of the Pacific to Trader Vic's and Don the Beachcomber's, this made an instant hit.

RUMAKI
[Makes 24 pieces]

12 slices bacon, cut in half	4 ounces water chestnuts
½ pound chicken livers, washed and dried	3 tablespoons soy sauce
	2 teaspoons brown sugar
Pinch ground ginger	

Cook bacon in blazer pan partially. Drain on paper towels.

Sauté livers in bacon grease only until firm but not cooked. Drain on paper towels. Cut livers into 24 bite-sized pieces.

Slice water chestnuts in 24 pieces.

Wrap a piece of liver and chestnut in ½ slice of bacon and secure with wooden toothpick.

Make a marinade of remaining ingredients and marinate the pieces, either in bowl or plastic bag, turning occasionally to coat pieces.

Preheat oven to 450° and place pieces on shallow baking pan. Place pan on rack and bake for 10 minutes, until bacon is crisp and livers are cooked but not dry.

Transfer to blazer pan over hot water, set at medium and keep warm while serving.

PRUMAKI
[Makes about 30 pieces]

1 pound large prunes	Pineapple Chutney (see below), chopped
Port wine to cover	
15 strips bacon	

Soak prunes overnight in wine; drain and remove pits.

Fill cavities with chutney. Wrap each prune in ½ bacon strip, fastening with wooden toothpicks.

Sauté prunes over high flame in blazer pan until bacon is crisp, half at a time. Drain on paper towels. Wipe out pan and put it over hot water, replacing prunes in pan to keep warm.

PINEAPPLE CHUTNEY
[Makes 4 8-ounce jars]

1 large pineapple, or 2 (1 pound, 13 ounce) cans pineapple
4 cups brown sugar
3 cups cider vinegar
2 cloves garlic
½ teaspoon whole cloves
1 pound seedless raisins
1 pound currants
1 pound blanched almonds, chopped, or broken-up walnuts
2 tablespoons peeled and chopped green ginger root
1½ teaspoons salt
½ teaspoon ground cinnamon
⅛ teaspoon fresh-ground pepper
½ teaspoon allspice

Trim and peel fresh pineapple; cut it or canned pineapple into small pieces. Combine all ingredients in 4-quart saucepan and boil until thick, about 20 minutes.

Remove garlic and cloves. Pour mixture into hot, sterilized jars and seal with paraffin immediately.

MONTE CRISTO ROUNDS
[Makes 24]

24 dollar-size rounds white bread
Butter
1½ cups ground lean boiled ham
Cream
Salt, cayenne, nutmeg and mustard to taste
24 round, thin slices Colby, Cheddar or Muenster cheese
Paprika

Toast bread on one side lightly. Spread untoasted side with butter, then cover with ham mixture, made by mixing ground ham with enough cream to make it spread easily, seasoned with salt, cayenne, nutmeg and mustard.

Cover with slice of cheese cut to fit (with rim of whisky glass or cookie cutter), sprinkle with paprika and toast in blazer pan over direct heat, covering until cheese gets melty.

ELECTRIC CHAFING DISH APPETIZERS

SHRIMP DIABLO
[Makes 2½ to 3 dozen]

This is a good recipe to prepare before your guests. It's simple and cooking times are short. The preparation can be done on a coffee table or service cart. Have the marinated shrimp drained and the butter and marinade ready for the pan. The aroma of the simmering marinade is a sure welcome to guests. Have plenty of party picks or skewers and paper plates and napkins ready.

Marinade

½ cup dry white wine	sauce
2 tablespoons lemon juice	1 teaspoon dry mustard
2 cloves garlic, minced	½ teaspoon salt
2 teaspoons Worcestershire	¼ teaspoon Tabasco sauce

2 pounds cooked, cleaned	¼ cup parsley, chopped
jumbo shrimp	Juice of ½ lemon or 1
2 tablespoons butter	tablespoon lemon juice
6 lemon slices, cut in half	

Blend wine and seasonings for marinade. Pour over shrimp and marinate for several hours or overnight. Thoroughly drain shrimp, reserving marinade.

Melt butter in blazer pan of electric chafing dish at high, add reserved marinade and cook, stirring occasionally, until reduced to about 2 tablespoons. Add shrimp and heat about 2 minutes, stirring constantly to coat shrimp. Sprinkle on parsley and lemon juice, stir lightly. Garnish with lemon slices around inside of blazer pan.

Place over hot water bath and keep warm at medium setting for serving.

Serve as an unusual appetizer

CAULIFLOWER A LA GRECQUE
[Serves 6]

⅓ cup water	1 head cauliflower, in
⅓ cup dry white wine	flowerets
¼ cup oil	1 tablespoon cornstarch
1 clove garlic, crushed	2 tablespoons water
½ teaspoon salt	1 tablespoon chopped
½ teaspoon dill weed	parsley
¼ teaspoon white pepper	1 tablespoon shredded lime
	peel

Put water, wine, oil and seasonings into blazer pan of electric chafing dish. Bring to a boil at high, add cauliflower. Reheat to boiling and cook uncovered for 7 minutes.

Blend cornstarch and water, add to cauliflower and cook, stirring constantly until thickened. Garnish with chopped parsley and shredded lime peel. Place over hot water bath and keep warm at medium setting.

RUBY HAM BALLS
[Makes 4 to 5 dozen]

2 slices fresh bread, finely	Dash nutmeg
crumbed	Dash ginger
3 tablespoons milk	Dash pepper
1 pound fresh lean pork,	2 tablespoons butter or
finely ground	margarine
½ pound cooked ham, finely	2 tablespoons vegetable oil
ground	1 cup Burgundy wine
1 egg slightly beaten	1 8½-ounce can crushed
2 teaspoons dry mustard	pineapple
1 teaspoon basil leaves	1 tablespoon cornstarch
¼ teaspoon paprika	1 tablespoon water

In large mixing bowl combine crumbs and milk and let stand 5 minutes.

Add pork, ham, egg and seasonings. Mix well. Shape mixture into 1-inch balls and chill for 30 minutes.

Heat butter and oil in large skillet on range, add about half of meat balls and sauté until golden brown. Cook about 5 minutes. Remove from pan and drain on absorbent paper. Cook remaining meat balls.

To serve, heat wine in blazer pan of electric chafing dish at high. Add pineapple with syrup.

Mix cornstarch and water and add to wine mixture, stirring constantly until thickened. Add meat balls and heat to bubbly. Place over hot water bath and keep warm at medium setting. Serve with party picks.

Variation:

Wurst Appetizers—1 pound little sausages or little wieners can be substituted for meat balls.

A Soupçon of "Soup's On!"

You don't usually think of making soup in a chafing dish, but just because it is such an off-beat idea, it will make a hit. All you need is a top pan of sufficient capacity.

I know a good deal of the fascination of having a seafood soup or stew at the Oyster Bar in Grand Central Station in New York is the ceremony of watching it being made right in front of you (if you sit at the counter) in gas-fired chafing dishes attached to the edge of the bar. The cook works right there, heating the cream or milk, the oysters or lobster or crab or shrimp, with the butter, seasonings, etc., quickly creating the rich, savory-smelling concoction which he tops with another gob of butter and a sprinkle of paprika and then tilts the hinged chafing dish over to pour the stew into the bowl and set it before a rather drooling you.

In like manner if you catch a hungry group around the table, and, without too much time elapsing, cook up that Grand Central Oyster Stew—or any one of the 20 or so soup formulas that follow—you have a captive audience whose appetites are enhanced by the sight, smell and anticipation of the soup to come.

You will admit that half of these recipes are quite out of the ordinary. And the other half are, as they are titled, Swift and Simple.

A secret of the Grand Central Oyster Bar's oyster stew is that clam liquor is used instead of oyster liquor.

GRAND CENTRAL OYSTER STEW
[Serves 4]

2 dashes Worcestershire
   sauce
4 dashes paprika
4 dashes celery salt

12 pats of butter
2 dozen freshly-opened
   oysters
2 cups clam liquor

4 cups milk or (half-and-half)

In large blazer pan, place Worcestershire sauce, paprika, celery salt and 8 pats of butter; bring to boil. Add oysters and clam liquor and cook until edges of oysters curl. Add milk and bring to boil.

Pour into four bowls and top with a sprinkle of paprika and another pat of butter on each.

EGG RAG SOUP
[Serves 4]

2 pints rich chicken broth
1 teaspoon cornstarch
2 eggs

Salt and white pepper to
   taste
1 teaspoon parsley

Bring broth to a simmer in large blazer pan over direct heat, until small bubbles form. Mix cornstarch with a little of the broth and pour into soup to thicken. Cook until soup clears.

Beat eggs in a cup only enough to combine whites and yellows.

Hold cup about 4 inches above simmering broth and pour egg slowly in a thin stream with one hand, stirring soup constantly with the other. This should draw egg into long strands and filaments. Stop and start the pouring several times, so that soup does not cool below simmering point. Add salt and pepper and parsley, stir well, remove from heat and serve.

CRUMBY CONSOMME
[Serves 6]

3 eggs
10 tablespoons grated
    Parmesan cheese

3 pints chicken consommé
8 tablespoons toasted
    breadcrumbs

Beat eggs and half of the Parmesan in a bowl.

Bring broth to boiling point, pour breadcrumbs in, all at once, and keep boiling slowly for 2 or 3 minutes, so that the broth becomes thicker.

Pour eggs and cheese mixture in warmed blazer pan over hot water, and slowly add the broth, beating until well blended. Serve remaining Parmesan on the side.

SAVORY MUSHROOM BISQUE
[Serves 4 to 6]

¼ cup butter (½ stick)
1 pound fresh mushrooms,
    coarsely chopped
1 tablespoon grated onion
¼ cup flour

1 teaspoon salt
2 dashes seasoned pepper
3 cups milk
1 can chicken broth
Sherry

In top pan of chafing dish, melt butter and add mushrooms and onion. Sauté over direct medium flame. Blend in flour and seasonings. Stir in milk and broth; cook and stir a few minutes until thickened. Add sherry to taste (about ¼ to ⅓ cup) and serve at once.

CANADIAN CHEESE BISQUE
[Serves 4]

1 tablespoon butter
1 tablespoon flour
¼ pound sharp Cheddar
    cheese, grated
1 pint clear chicken broth
2 teaspoons fine-minced
    celery
1 teaspoon fine-minced
    carrot

Pinch white pepper
¼ teaspoon salt
¼ teaspoon Worcestershire
    sauce
2 teaspoons butter
2 teaspoons minced green
    pepper
½ cup ale

Blend flour and butter in blazer pan over medium heat until smooth. Add cheese and stir until smooth again.

In small saucepan simmer vegetables in chicken broth until tender. Add to cheese mixture and whip until smooth. Add pepper, salt and Worcestershire. Keep warm.

In separate pan, sauté green pepper in butter, then add to above.

Warm ale slightly and just before serving, add ale to soup and mix well.

CHEDDAR CHEESE SOUP
[Serves 4]

1 small onion, fine-chopped
1 ounce (2 tablespoons) butter
1 quart milk
2 eggs, slightly beaten

3 ounces grated Cheddar cheese
Salt, pepper and grated nutmeg

In bottom of large skillet or blazer pan, fry onion in butter without browning; add milk and when nearly boiling, stir in eggs and cheese and season to taste. Do not boil again. Serve with rounds of French bread, toasted in oven.

ASPARAGUS CHEESE SOUP
[Serves 4 to 6]

3 tablespoons butter
2 tablespoons flour
Salt and white pepper
2 cups milk at room temperature
2 cups chicken broth, or 3

chicken consommé cubes dissolved in 2 cups hot water
1 cup cooked asparagus, chopped
1½ cups grated Cheddar cheese

Melt butter in large blazer pan over low heat. Remove and add flour and liberal seasonings, blending well. Add milk gradually until well blended. Then add chicken broth.

Return to low heat and stir until smooth and thick; add asparagus and heat again; add cheese and stir until melted and well blended.

Garnish with thin strips of pimiento or chopped chives or slivers of pistachio nuts.

SENEGALESE SOUP
[Serves 6]

2 cans condensed cream of chicken soup
1 can clear chicken broth
2 tablespoons curry powder

½ teaspoon salt
¼ teaspoon paprika
2 drops Tabasco sauce
½ pint cream

In large blazer pan over flame blend the soup and broth and bring to boil. Mix in curry, salt, paprika and Tabasco, reduce heat and simmer 5 minutes.

Remove pan from heat, blend in cream and serve.

Top each serving with sprinkle of mint leaves, or parsley and ¼ teaspoon minced peanuts.

This is a soup which can be chilled several hours and served very cold.

LONDON CREAM SOUP
[Serves 4]

1 quart light cream
4 ounces breadcrumbs
4 egg yolks

5 ounces milk
½ teaspoon grated nutmeg
Juice of 1 lemon

1 cup boiled rice

Cook cream in blazer pan with breadcrumbs over low heat for 10 minutes; remove and force through sieve. Return to pan with egg yolks which have been beaten lightly with the milk. Add nutmeg and lemon juice and beat over simmering heat until soup is thick and creamy. Just before ladling out, add rice and mix well.

MARDI GRAS GUMBO
[Serves 6 to 8]

1 can condensed chicken
  gumbo soup
1 can condensed tomato
  soup

1½ soup cans hot water
1 cup flaked crabmeat, or
  1 7-ounce can
2 tablespoons sherry

2 cups hot cooked rice

In large blazer pan over boiling water combine all ingredients except rice and heat, stirring occasionally, until steaming.

Line soup tureen or large bowl with the cooked rice and pour in the soup.

HUNGARIAN GOULASH SOUP
[Serves 4]

2 tablespoons butter or
  margarine
⅓ cup minced green pepper
½ teaspoon paprika
1 can condensed tomato

soup
1 soup can water
1 cup cubed cooked beef
½ teaspoon caraway seed
2 cups hot noodles

Melt butter in top pan of chafing dish and cook pepper and paprika until pepper is tender.

Add rest of ingredients, except noodles, and heat together, stirring often until heated through. Simmer over low flame 5 minutes.

Either stir noodles in, or serve in soup plates and pour soup over.

This Danish specialty can be prepared half way in advance, then finished in chafing dish while guests are nibbling appetizers and imbibing their cocktails.

APPLE SOUP
[Serves 8 to 10]

4 tart unpeeled apples, cored and quartered	½ teaspoon salt
	3 tablespoons cornstarch
4 cups water	¼ cup water
2 tablespoons grated lemon peel	5 teaspoons sugar, more or less
¾ teaspoon cinnamon	⅓ cup sherry

Combine apples and 2 cups water; cook in saucepan at a boil until soft. Add lemon peel and cinnamon. Remove to container of electric blender and process at high speed 5 seconds.

Pour back into pan, add other 2 cups of water and salt.

Blend cornstarch with ¼ cup water, add to soup and cook, stirring constantly until slightly thickened and clear. Keep warm.

When ready for chafing dish, pour into blazer pan over boiling water and cook 10 minutes more, stirring occasionally. Then add sugar and sherry; cook 2 minutes longer and serve hot.

Amount of sugar depends on tartness of the apples, but soup should have tart flavor.

SWIFT AND SIMPLE SOUPS

Prowling through a portfolio of Campbell soup suggestions, I've selected the top ten as simply and quickly made potages which can be done in a chafing dish. If you use hot water, you will speed up the process.

SPLIT PEA AND TOMATO SOUP
[Serves 4 to 6]

1 can condensed split pea with ham soup	1 can condensed tomato soup
	1 cup milk
1 cup water	

Blend soups in blazer pan. Place over medium heat and gradually stir in milk and water. Heat through but do not boil, stirring frequently.

SALMON SOUP
[Serves 4]

1 tablespoon butter or margarine	1 can condensed cream of vegetable soup
½ cup thin-sliced cucumber	1 cup water
2 tablespoons minced onion	1 8-ounce can salmon, drained and flaked
⅛ teaspoon minced dill leaves	

⅓ cup sour cream

Melt butter in blazer pan and cook cucumber, onion and dill until partially tender. Blend in remaining ingredients and heat, but do not boil, stirring often.

HOT DOG SOUP
[Serves 2 to 3]

1 tablespoon butter or margarine	2 tablespoons minced onion
2 hot dogs, sliced thin	1 can condensed tomato-rice soup

1 soup can water

Sizzle butter in blazer pan over direct heat. Add hot dogs and onion and brown briskly. Add soup and water; heat through, stirring often.

Double quantities for 4 to 6.

LOBSTER-MUSHROOM SOUP
[Serves 6 to 8]

2 tablespoons butter or
   margarine
¼ cup chopped onion
1 can condensed cream of
   mushroom soup
1 can condensed cream of
   celery soup
1 soup can milk

1 soup can water
1 cup flaked cooked lobster,
   or 1 6½-ounce can,
   drained
2 tablespoons chopped
   parsley
Dash pepper
Dash paprika

Melt butter in chafing dish blazer pan and cook onion until tender. Blend in soups and remaining ingredients. Heat, stirring often, garnishing each serving with more paprika.

Variations: Instead of lobster, use shrimp, crab, salmon or tuna.

SWISS POTATO SOUP
[Serves 6]

2 cans frozen condensed
   cream of potato soup,
   thawed
2 soup cans milk

¼ teaspoon dry mustard
1 cup diced Emmentaler
   cheese
1 tablespoon minced parsley

Combine soup, milk and mustard, stirring well with wooden spoon until heated, using blazer pan over medium heat. Add cheese and heat, stirring just until cheese melts. Sprinkle parsley over.

For a thinner soup, use 1 can milk and 1 can water.

LITTLE PIG AND BEAN SOUP
[Serves 4 to 6]

4 ounces (¼ pound) little
   sausage links in ½-inch
   slices
1 can condensed bean with
   bacon soup
1 soup can water
1 cup diced red apple

Brown sausage in blazer pan over medium heat; pour off drippings. Blend in soup and water, heating through while stirring. Top each serving with apple dice.

EASY MINESTRONE
[Serves 6 to 8]

½ cup Italian sausage, cut in thin rounds

2 cans condensed minestrone soup

1 can condensed tomato soup

3 soup cans water

Croutons or breadsticks

In blazer pan over medium heat, brown sausage rounds, then drain off fat. Add the soups and water and heat, stirring often until heated through. Serve, topped with croutons or broken bits of breadsticks.

CHICKEN CORN CHOWDER
[Serves 6 to 8]

1 can condensed cream of chicken soup

2 soup cans milk

1 can condensed chicken noodle soup

1 1-pound can cream-style corn

1 cup diced cooked chicken or 1 5-ounce can boned chicken

Blend cream of chicken soup and milk in blazer pan of chafing dish over boiling water. Add remaining ingredients and heat through, but do not boil.

FRANK 'N' BEAN SOUP
[Serves 4 or 5]

1 tablespoon butter or margarine

3 frankfurters, thin-sliced

1 can condensed bean with

bacon soup

1 can green pea soup

1 soup can milk

1 soup can water

In blazer pan of chafing dish brown frankfurter slices lightly in butter, then blend in remaining ingredients and heat well, but do not boil.

A cup of diced, cooked carrots may also be added.

LEFTOVER SOUP
[Serves 2 to 6]

1 cup whatever meat on hand, cut in strips

2 tablespoons butter or margarine

2 cans any condensed or frozen soup, or mixed

2 soup cans milk or water, depending on soup

1 cup cooked vegetables

In blazer pan cook meat in butter until lightly browned. Add remaining ingredients and heat well, stirring often.

Breaking the Fast...Having a Bunch For Brunch

Appetizers and soups being taken care of in previous sections, let us skip back to the beginning of the day and pay a little attention to breakfast.

Admittedly, on weekdays, with the mad scramble to get to work or school, a chafing dish stands little chance of getting much attention from the family.

Which is not as it should be.

You can whip up such tasty, hot temptations with your chafing dish that you can start the family getting to table 10 or 15 minutes earlier, just to enjoy a delicious opening-of-the-day meal.

Not only delicious, but nutritious. One of the most exhaustive surveys ever undertaken by the Department of Agriculture examined 10,000 people of all ages, occupations and localities about their breakfast-eating habits. Conclusion: Those who had eaten a hearty breakfast lasted best through the day; the ones who either skipped or skimped on their first meal started to get that dragged-out feeling along about 3 or 4 P.M. And no wonder—they simply had run out of fuel.

The following recipes are especially practicable for special occasions—especially Sunday brunch, wedding breakfasts, graduation celebrations, Mah-Jongg parties, or any far-out excuse you may dream up.

Note that I have included Egg Dishes, Pastas, Fried Cheese, and Pancakes and Crêpes of the non-sweet kind, since these all fit in with the other breakfast-brunch assortment. It also enables me to skip a Lunch Section, since these all can be used at that time; and since you will encounter, later, a Main Dish Section, full of recipes which can be used at luncheon as well as dinner—or at midnight snack time, for that matter.

Here is a program for a pleasant Sunday Brunch:

TOMATO FRAPPE

Pour tomato juice cocktail for four into tray used for ice-cubes and freeze until slushy. Serve in chilled glasses with lemon slices.

HAM BALLS IN MUSTARD SAUCE
[Serves 4]

2 eggs, beaten	½ teaspoon turmeric
2 cups ground cooked ham	¾ cup butter or margarine
4 hard-cooked eggs, minced	½ cup flour
2 tablespoons minced onion	⅓ cup Dijon mustard
1 teaspoon celery seed	4 cups milk

Mix eggs in medium bowl with ham, hard-cooked eggs, onion, celery seed and turmeric. Shape into about 3 dozen small balls, about 1 inch in diameter.

Heat 2 tablespoons of the butter in skillet or blazer pan and lightly brown half the ham balls; remove to warm dish.

Repeat with remaining balls, adding additional 2 tablespoons of butter. Remove ham balls.

Melt remaining ½ cup butter, and stir in flour and mustard. Gradually add in milk and cook, stirring constantly until sauce thickens and comes to a boil. Add ham balls and sauce, place blazer pan over boiling water and heat through. Serve over hot waffles. Finish with raspberry ice with crème de menthe and coffee.

A second Sunday Brunch menu. It looks elaborate but is rather simple to prepare. Start with minted melon balls, then

CHICKEN LIVERS SUPERB
[Serves 8]

½ cup butter or margarine
2 cups diced cooked ham
2 cups quartered fresh
  mushrooms
2 pounds chicken livers, cut
  in half
⅔ cup flour
⅔ cup chopped onion

2 cups chicken broth
1½ cups dry Madeira or
  Marsala
2 teaspoons salt
½ teaspoon fresh-ground
  pepper
¼ cup finely chopped
  parsley or tarragon

½ cup sour cream

Heat ¼ cup of the butter in large skillet; add ham and mushrooms; cook until mushrooms are tender.

Remove to chafing dish blazer pan over boiling water. Dust chicken livers with the flour.

Heat remaining ¼ cup butter in skillet. Add chicken livers and onion. Cook until livers are lightly browned on all sides. Add broth, wine, salt and pepper and simmer until chicken livers are done, 5 to 7 minutes.

Remove from heat; stir in sour cream. Pour mixture over ham and mushrooms in chafing dish. Blend gently. Sprinkle with parsley or tarragon. Keep warm. Serve with hot fluffy rice and herb biscuits. For dessert, mocha mousse with chocolate sauce and coffee.

Here is a third full-dress Brunch for Sundays and in this case it is the dessert which is prepared in the chafing dish.

ICED BOUILLON

Serve bouillon over ice cubes in cups, garnished with parsley and thin slices of lemon.

Follow with artichoke heart omelets, grilled tomatoes and hot French bread. For dessert

HOT FRUIT COMPOTE
[Serves 6 or 7]

1½ cups dried apricots
¼ cup currants
2 tablespoons slivered candied ginger
2 tablespoons grenadine syrup
2 cups water

1 1-pound 14-ounce can pear halves, drained
¼ cup toasted, slivered almonds
½ cup fluffy marshmallow crème

In blazer pan of chafing dish over direct flame, simmer apricots, currants and ginger in grenadine and water 10 minutes. Add pears, sprinkle almonds all over. In hollow of each pear half put 1 tablespoon marshmallow crème. Heat until pears are warm and marshmallow begins to melt. Serve butter cookies and coffee.

Variation: Fresh fruit may be substituted for dried apricots and seedless grapes for the currants. Less cooking time would be required.

Florence Foreman Rypinski, who divides her year between California and Honolulu, wrote out this very successful recipe of hers while flying over the Pacific.

HAWAIIAN BRUNCH
[Serves 8]

Deviled Eggs

12 hard-cooked eggs
1 cup mayonnaise

3 tablespoons prepared mustard

Salt and pepper to taste

Cut eggs in half, lengthwise, remove yolks and put them through fine sieve. Beat until they become paste. Add mayonnaise, mustard and salt and pepper. Beat until very creamy and smooth. Fill egg-white halves generously.

Cream Sauce (1 pint):

2 tablespoons butter
2 tablespoons minced onion
2 tablespoons flour
2 cups hot milk
1½ teaspoons curry powder

Pinch salt
1 cup precooked ham in
small dice
½ cup chopped macadamia
nuts

Melt butter in saucepan and brown onions. Add flour and blend well until lumps disappear. Add milk and blend well again. Add curry powder, salt and pepper and stir. Cook 15 minutes. Strain through fine sieve. Add ham and cook 5 minutes longer.

Arrange Deviled Egg halves in chafing dish. Cover them with the sauce and sprinkle chopped nuts over. Heat through and serve.

You don't usually think of dessert with breakfast, but when it's a special occasion, like breaking your fast at Brennan's fancy restaurant in New Orleans, that occasion is usually marked with a posh sweet, like

BANANAS FOSTER
[Serves 2]

¼ cup packed brown sugar
2 tablespoons butter
2 ripe bananas, peeled and
sliced lengthwise

Dash cinnamon
2 tablespoons banana
liqueur
¼ cup light rum

Melt sugar and butter in flat chafing dish or suzette pan over direct flame. Add bananas and sauté until tender. Sprinkle with cinnamon. Pour in banana liqueur and warm rum. Set ablaze. Using long-handled silver spoon, baste with warm liquid until flame burns out. Serve immediately.

You need serve no fruit at breakfast if you cook these Norwegian Pancakes for your family or guests. They make fine light desserts, too.

NORWEGIAN APPLE PANCAKES
[Makes 24 4-inch pancakes]

1 cup sour cream	1 tablespoon sugar
1 cup small curd cottage	¾ teaspoon salt
cheese	1½ cups raw apple, diced
4 eggs	small
¾ cup sifted flour	Butter

Syrup

Combine sour cream and cheese, place together with eggs, flour, sugar and salt in blender container or mixer bowl and whirl until well mixed. Add apple.

Bake on hot buttered blazer pan until bubbles break on surface, then turn and bake until golden brown.

Serve with butter and syrup.

Variation:

Norwegian Blueberry Pancakes: Substitute 1 cup fresh blueberries, or canned or frozen and drained, for the apples.

EYE-OPENER
[Serves 4 to 6]

8 eggs	4 apples, cored, pared and in
Salt	thin slices
Confectioners' sugar	3 tablespoons applejack or
Butter	calvados

Fine granulated sugar

Beat eggs with salt and confectioners' sugar to taste. Bring eggs, sugars, and apples to table in separate containers.

In blazer pan over direct heat melt butter for omelet, pour in egg mixture and make omelet. When cooked, sprinkle surface with granulated sugar and cover with apple slices. Fold omelet over and sprinkle with confectioners' sugar.

Heat applejack in small pan or ladle, set afire and pour over omelet.

When flames die down, serve immediately on warmed plates, pouring any sauce remaining over portions.

This is an effective breakfast dish, combining fruit and eggs in a spectacular blaze calculated to bring awake any sleepyheads.

This makes a memorable Sunday breakfast or brunch dish.

HEAVENLY HASH
[Serves 6]

6 cups heavy cream
3 cups fine-cut cooked
   chicken breasts
4 egg yolks, beaten

½ cup warm sherry or
   Marsala wine
Salt and white pepper
French Toast (see below)

In blazer pan over direct heat, bring cream to boil; add chicken and simmer slowly 5 minutes.

Thicken sauce by adding egg yolks to sherry, then mix in 2 tablespoons of the hot cream sauce. Pour all into hot sauce, stirring and mixing well. Bring almost to a boil, agitating pan to prevent sticking. Season to taste and serve over French Toast.

FRENCH TOAST
[Serves 6]

2 eggs
½ teaspoon salt
½ cup milk

1 tablespoon dark rum
6 slices bread
Butter

In one bowl beat eggs and salt slightly.

In second bowl or dish, mix together milk and rum.

Soak bread slices first in milk, then in egg mixture, then fry on both sides in hot butter in skillet. Keep hot until ready to serve on hot plates.

If you received three chafing dishes as wedding presents, or accumulated them in less difficult manner—or have a

3 compartment blazer pan—here is an interesting breakfast, brunch . . . or even late supper dish. For audience participation, you might assign a different pan as the responsibility of one or a group of guests.

CHICKEN LIVERS WITH APPLES AND ONIONS
[Serves 6]

6 tablespoons butter	1½ Bermuda onions, sliced in
24 chicken livers	rings
1 teaspoon salt	Parsley
¼ teaspoon paprika	12 apple slices ½-inch thick
4 tablespoons flour	Sugar and cinnamon

Melt 2 tablespoons butter in each of three blazer pans over moderate heat. Simultaneously, cook livers, onions, and apples, each in its own pan, thus:

Livers: Drain, cut in half, shake in bag with salt, paprika and flour.

Sauté until well-browned and blood stops running.

Onions: Sauté until medium-brown, sprinkle with salt and pepper; add 2 tablespoons water, parsley; then simmer until ready to serve.

Apples: Fry over high heat, sprinkle with sugar and cinnamon to glaze, turning 2 or 3 times until soft and browned.

Serve in luncheon plates with 2 apple slices on bottoms, livers on apples and onions on top.

HONEY-HONEY TOAST
[Serves 4]

2 eggs	¼ teaspoon salt
¼ cup honey	8 slices bread
¼ cup milk	Butter or margarine
Honey Sauce (see below)	

Beat eggs slightly and combine with honey, milk and salt; blend well. Dip bread slices in mixture on both sides, soaking well.

Melt butter in blazer pan over direct heat and cook bread until golden brown on both sides. Serve with Honey Sauce.

HONEY SAUCE

1 cup honey	margarine
2 tablespoons butter or	2 tablespoons lemon juice

Combine the ingredients, and heat, stirring constantly. Serve over toast.

ON THE BEATING OF EGGS

Whole eggs are either *beaten lightly* to blend the white and the yellow thoroughly, or they are *well beaten* to incorporate air, increasing the bulk.

Egg yolks are either *beaten until thoroughly blended* or *until thick and pale.*

Egg whites are 1) *beaten until light,* that is until frothy and beginning to thicken, but will not hold their shape, or 2) *until stiff,* which is when the white will stand in peaks when the beater is taken out. When *stiff* is called for, stop before the whites become 3) *dry beaten,* when they lose moisture and some of their lightness.

Don't keep egg whites standing after beating or the air will dissipate and they will become liquid again. They cannot be rebeaten.

ALABAMA EGGS
[Serves 1]

1 slice bread	1 egg
Butter or bacon fat	Salt and pepper to taste

With small cookie cutter or whiskey glass rim, cut hole in center of bread slice.

Heat butter or fat to lukewarm or medium. Put in bread. Break egg carefully in center of hole. Cook to golden brown on bottom; flip or turn carefully over and cook to desired doneness.

Can be served with ham, bacon or sausage.

To be a good chafing dish chef, you must know when to put it on and when to take it off—and when to put it on the plates.

EGGS ALLA DAMARINI
[Serves 4]

1 tablespoon butter
2 tablespoons chopped green pepper
1 cup tomatoes

1 teaspoon sugar
1 teaspoon salt
1 knife-tip paprika
3 eggs

In blazer pan or chafing dish, over direct heat, melt butter, stir in pepper and cook 4 minutes. Add tomatoes, sugar, salt, and paprika. Stir and heat well.

Place pan over hot water pan and pour in unbeaten eggs. Cook without stirring until whites are coagulated, then break up with fork and continue cooking until done to taste. Place slices of toast on plates and divide egg mixture evenly.

This was a favorite dish of my friend, the late creator of "Fibber McGee and Molly" and "The Halls of Ivy."

SCRAMBLED EGGS A LA DON QUINN
[Serves 2]

3 eggs
Salt
3 tablespoons cream
2 tablespoons butter
3 tablespoons diced ham

1 teaspoon chopped green pepper
1 teaspoon minced pimiento
1/2 cup fresh corn, sautéed in butter

4 little pork sausages

Beat eggs well in small mixing bowl with salt to taste and cream.

Heat butter in blazer pan over medium-high flame; add ham, green pepper and pimiento; sauté 1 minute; add eggs, stirring very lightly while shaking pan until eggs reach soft stage.

Sauté corn and keep hot.

Heap eggs on heated serving plate, arranging in neat

circle. Form border of hot corn around eggs. Place very hot sausages, well browned, on top of eggs. Serve immediately.

SCRAMBLED EGGS A LA DEAUVILLE
[Serves 4]

6 eggs, well beaten	5 tablespoons butter
Pinch dill	¼ pound cooked crabmeat,
Pinch chopped chives	lobster meat or shrimp,
Pinch nutmeg	in small pieces
Salt and pepper to taste	Fresh-ground pepper

Mix eggs, dill, chives, nutmeg and salt and pepper until well blended.

Melt 4 tablespoons of the butter in blazer pan of chafing dish over medium direct flame. When hot but not brown, spoon 1 tablespoon of the butter into egg mixture and stir. Then add egg mixture to blazer pan and cook over low flame, stirring with wooden spoon continuously until starting to solidify. Add remaining tablespoon butter and continue stirring until eggs are light and very soft. Add seafood, a grind of pepper, heat through and serve at once.

Constance Carr, who wrote the one-gal cookbook, *Lazy Lady Lunches,* contributed this recipe from the days of '49.

HANGTOWN SCRAMBLE
[Serves 4]

3 slices bacon	peppers, sliced thin
16 oysters, fresh or canned	2 tablespoons chili sauce
4 small hot green Mexican	3 eggs

Cook bacon in chafing dish until crisp, remove to plate and crumble.

Pour out most of bacon fat, leaving just enough to fry other ingredients. Fry oysters until edges curl, then cut into quarters. Add peppers, chili sauce and eggs, all together, along with crumbled bacon, and scramble together until eggs have coagulated.

Serve hot on buttered toast or with potato chips.

Another version, done as an omelet.

HANGTOWN FRY
[Serves 4]

1 12-ounce jar fresh, small oysters	7 eggs
Salt and fresh-ground pepper	2 tablespoons butter
Cracker meal	4 slices bacon, cut into as many pieces as there are oysters

¼ cup milk

Salt and pepper oysters. Dip each in cracker meal, then in 1 egg, beaten, then in cracker meal again.

Heat butter in large blazer pan and fry oysters gently until golden brown on one side.

Meanwhile fry bacon separately and drain.

Beat 6 remaining eggs with milk, salt and pepper to taste.

When oysters are browned, turn them over. Top each with a piece of bacon. Pour in egg mixture and cook gently until set. Fold in half and serve on hot platter with French fries.

If you cook them one at a time—

HANGTOWN OMELET
[Serves 1]

2 eggs, well-beaten	1 teaspoon minced pimiento
Salt to taste	Fresh-ground pepper
2 tablespoons butter	3 breaded oysters, fried in butter
1 tablespoon minced green pepper	2 slices crisp bacon
1 teaspoon minced green onion	Watercress

Whip eggs with salt in mixing bowl.

Heat butter in blazer pan and sauté green pepper, onion and pimiento, stirring constantly for 90 seconds; add eggs and blend well. Salt and pepper to taste. Add oysters. Make a flat omelet, slightly browned on both sides by turning carefully.

Transfer to hot serving plate; make an X with bacon; garnish with watercress and serve at once.

WESTERN OMELET
[Serves 4]

2 tablespoons butter, margarine or shortening	4 eggs, slightly beaten
¼ cup chopped green pepper	½ cup diced cooked tongue or ham
2 tablespoons chopped onion	Salt and pepper to taste

Melt butter in blazer pan or crêpes pan and cook pepper and onion until soft.

Blend together eggs, tongue and salt and pepper. Add to pan and stir gently, cooking over low heat until firm.
Variation:

Tenderfoot Omelet: Proceed as above, except eliminate onions.

SPANISH OMELET
[Serves 2]

2 small tomatoes	1 ounce smoked garlic sausage
1 small onion	4 eggs
1 tablespoon French-cut beans, cooked	1 tablespoon cooked peas
1 medium potato, cooked	2 teaspoons olive oil
	Salt and pepper to taste

Peel tomatoes, remove seeds, and chop. Chop onion and French beans, dice potato and sausage.

Beat eggs lightly, add vegetables, sausage, peas, salt and pepper.

Melt oil in omelet or blazer pan, pour in egg mixture and cook quickly for 3 minutes. Turn carefully and brown other side.

Slide out without folding onto a hot plate.

CREOLE EGGS
[Serves 4]

3 tablespoons butter
1 tablespoon minced onion
2 thin-sliced mushroom caps
1 cup peeled, seeded, drained
    tomatoes

1 tablespoon chopped capers
Salt to taste
Dash Tabasco sauce
Triangles of toasted
    buttered rye bread

6 eggs, lightly beaten

Melt butter in blazer pan over direct flame. Add onion and mushrooms and cook until they begin to brown. Add tomatoes and cook 10 minutes. Remove and place pan over boiling water.

Add capers, salt and Tabasco. Mix well.

Add eggs and cook, stirring gently. Pour over toasted rye bread on heated plates.

EGG HUBBLE-BUBBLE
[Serves 4 or 5]

6 ounces cooked potatoes
4 small tomatoes
4 ounces mushrooms
2 ounces butter

4 ounces cooked peas or
    broad beans
2 ounces Cheddar cheese,
    grated

6 eggs

Dice potatoes into 1-inch pieces.

Peel and quarter tomatoes and mushrooms.

Melt butter in blazer pan and fry potatoes until well browned. Fry tomatoes and mushrooms lightly, so they are just brown. Add peas or beans and heat very gently, stirring as little as possible.

Beat the eggs lightly; add salt and pepper to taste and pour over vegetables. Sprinkle cheese over top. Cover with lid and cook gently until just set. Serve immediately.

OEUFS A L'ESTRAGON
[Serves 4]

4 tablespoons butter	2 tablespoons tarragon
8 eggs	vinegar

In blazer pan over direct flame, brown butter. When it foams, add unbeaten eggs one at a time and cut heat to half (or place pan over hot water). When eggs are half cooked, add vinegar. Cover tightly for 2 minutes, until yolks are coated with white and vinegar evaporates.

PASTAS

Surely one of the most romantically luxurious hotels in the world is the Gritti Palace, on the Grand Canal in Venice. This is not only my opinion, but that of other writers, such as W. Somerset Maugham and Ernest Hemingway, to name but two, even though they didn't write about food.

Pierre Barrelet, the manager, has favored me with the following favorite recipe of the hotel, which I am passing on to you.

FETTUCCINE ALLA GRITTI
[Serves 4]

4 ounces (1 stick) butter	homemade if possible,
4 tablespoons boiled	half-cooked
chopped ham	⅔ cup cream
4 tablespoons prosciutto,	Fresh-ground pepper to
chopped	taste
8 ounces (1 package) thin	4 ounces (1 cup) grated
egg noodles, or	Parmesan cheese
¾ cup cooked tiny peas	

Melt butter in chafing dish blazer pan over brisk flame; add cooked and raw ham and "beat it up," i.e. stir vigorously until hot and soft. Add noodles and blend until they are hot. Add cream and stir constantly until butter, ham and cream are reduced to a thick sauce. Season with pepper. Then add peas. Serve with Parmesan.

Armando Armanni, the affable and popular managing director of the Excelsior Hotel, Rome, sent me this recipe.

SPAGHETTI ALL'ARRABBIATA
[Serves 6]

2 pounds spaghetti	½ pound chopped bacon
Salt	4 ounces dry white wine
4 tablespoons chopped onions	1¾ pounds peeled tomatoes
	Cayenne pepper
4 tablespoons olive oil	2½ ounces Parmesan cheese

Cook spaghetti in plenty of boiling water with a pinch of salt for 8 minutes; drain and keep warm.

Meanwhile sauté onions in olive oil in skillet or saucepan until they are browned. Add bacon and cook 3 minutes more. Pour in the wine and let it boil down for 4 minutes. Add tomatoes, cayenne and a pinch of salt and cook until sauce is thick.

Then transfer spaghetti to blazer pan of chafing dish over boiling water, blend in sauce, sprinkle with Parmesan and serve immediately.

QUADRETTINI A LA FELICE EARLEY
[Serves 6]

4 ounces (1 stick) butter	8 ounces quadrettini (little square noodles), cooked *al dente* [1]
¼ pound prosciutto	
1 cup spinach, cooked, drained and chopped	
Salt and pepper	½ cup grated Parmesan cheese
2 tablespoons butter	

In blazer pan, melt butter. Chop prosciutto into bits and sauté in butter over low heat until transparent. Add spinach, salt and pepper and cook 4 minutes longer. Add quadrettini, Parmesan and additional butter and toss thoroughly. Heat through and serve immediately.

---

[1] "To the tooth," i.e. not quite done.

From the world-famous Excelsior Hotel on the Via Veneto in Rome comes this dish and the following one.

BUCATINI EXCELSIOR
[Serves 6]

1½ pounds bucatini
½ pound thin-sliced ham or prosciutto, in small strips
¼ pound (1 stick) butter

3 egg yolks, beaten
4 tablespoons cream
4 tablespoons Parmesan cheese
Pinch fresh-ground pepper

Cook pasta in ample water with pinch of salt about 12 minutes. Drain.

In blazer pan over brisk flame, cook ham in butter while bucatini is cooking. As soon as bucatini is drained, cream, cheese and pepper, mix well, heat through and mix it in pan with ham, blending well. Add egg yolks, serve at once.

NOODLES VENETIAN STYLE
[Serves 6]

1⅓ pounds noodles, homemade if possible
1 cup cooked fresh peas

⅓ pound butter
5 tablespoons cream
2 ounces Parmesan cheese
Fresh-ground pepper

Cook noodles in plenty of very lightly salted boiling water for 8 or 9 minutes.

Drain and place in blazer pan of chafing dish with peas. Add butter and cream, mix well and heat through. Sprinkle with the cheese and a touch of pepper, mix well again and serve immediately.

"The chafing dish is hardly ever used in Sicilian regional dishes," writes Arthur Oliver from Palermo. "However, I have noted that the sauce for Spaghetti Maître d'Hôtel is frequently prepared at the table over a spirit lamp.

"This recipe is sufficient for 1 kilo (2.2 pounds) of spaghetti, enough to serve 8 people.

"The spaghetti is cooked in the kitchen 'al dente' and brought in at the last moment."

MAITRE D'HOTEL SAUCE FOR SPAGHETTI
[Serves 8]

4 tablespoons butter
¼ pound peeled and seeded
    tomatoes
½ pound cooked sliced

mushrooms
½ pound cooked ham, diced
1 cup cream
Salt and pepper to taste
Hot cooked spaghetti

Melt butter in blazer pan of chafing dish over boiling water; add tomatoes and simmer 4 minutes. Add all other ingredients, blend well and warm through.

Stir mixture into hot spaghetti, leaving some over to put on top of each plateful.

CHAFING DISH MACARONI AND CHEESE
[Serves 4 to 6]

1½ tablespoons butter or
    margarine
4 tablespoons minced onion

1 can condensed Cheddar
    cheese soup
½ cup milk
3 cups cooked macaroni

Melt butter in blazer pan and cook onion until tender. Blend in soup, then gradually add milk. Heat through, stirring often. Mix in macaroni and heat again, stirring. Serve hot on warm plates.

FRIED CHEESES

There are dozens of different soft French cheeses which can be fried in a chafing dish to make breakfast tidbits or hors d'oeuvre—or as a serving for 2.

FRENCH CHEESE, FRIED

1 small cheese (see list below)   Flour
Sugar   1 egg, beaten
Paprika   Breadcrumbs
                Butter

Cut soft, not too ripe cheese of about 8 inches in half, leaving crust on. Do not cut cheese weighing 3 to 5 ounces. Sprinkle all over first with sugar, then paprika, dredge in flour, dip in egg then cover with breadcrumbs.

Heat a couple tablespoons of butter in blazer pan of chafing dish over medium flame and fry cheese quickly to a golden brown. Serve hot.

Cheese List: Among the cheeses which can be fried, and their weights: Bondon, 7 ounces; Briard, 8 ounces; Brie, 8 ounces; Camembert, 8 ounces; Carre de l'Est, 6 ounces; Coulommiers, 10 ounces; Excelsior, 2 3-ounce packages; Fromage Four Seasons, 7 ounces; Le Cigone, 8 ounces; Le Notre Dame, 8 ounces; Monsieur Fromage, 2 5-ounce packages; Non Non, 2 5-ounce packages; Noisette de Leice, 8 ounces; Petite Français, 2 3-ounce packages; Pont l'Evèque Fermier, 10 ounces; Roquefort, ½ pound; Valencay, 6 ounces.

GRUYERE CROQUETTES
[Serves 4]

Béchamel Sauce (see below)   2 egg yolks
¼ pound Gruyère cheese,   ⅓ cup flour
   grated   Olive oil

To hot Béchamel add Gruyère cheese, mixing well. Remove from heat and mix in egg yolks. Let cool. After mixture is cool, take by spoonfuls and roll in flour and fry in hot olive oil in blazer pan on all sides.

BECHAMEL SAUCE
[Makes 2 cups]

2 ounces butter
1/4 pound flour

1 pint milk
Pinch salt and paprika

Melt butter, blend in flour, add milk, salt and paprika, and mix well, all in blazer pan or skillet over medium flame. When it boils it is ready to be used as above.

FRIED MOZZARELLA
[Serves 4 to 6]

1 pound Mozzarella cheese
1/2 cup flour
2 eggs, slightly beaten

Salt and pepper
1 cup breadcrumbs
1 cup olive oil

Cut cheese into 1-inch cubes, roll in flour.

Season eggs to taste, beat; dip cheese in egg, roll in breadcrumbs, again in egg and again in breadcrumbs.

Fry in hot olive oil in blazer pan just long enough for breadcrumbs to turn golden color. Serve hot.

PANCAKES FOR BREAKFAST—OR ANY TIME

DOLLAR HOT CAKES
[Makes 1 quart batter]

1 egg
1/4 teaspoon salt
1 1/2 teaspoons sugar
3/4 teaspoon vanilla
1 1/2 pints milk
1/2 teaspoon baking powder

1 small package pancake flour (slightly less than 1 lb.)
1 tablespoon melted butter or salad oil

Beat egg, salt, sugar, and vanilla well together. Add milk, baking powder, and pancake flour, mixing well together.

Then add melted butter or salad oil and blend. This batter is best if it stands overnight. Next day, if too heavy for thin cakes, add more milk.

Fry small cakes in blazer pan over medium flame. Serve with little pork sausages, blanched in milk and fried in butter.

FLUFFY PANCAKES
[Makes 15]

3 eggs, separated
1⅔ cups buttermilk
1 teaspoon soda
1½ cups sifted all-purpose
    flour

1 tablespoon sugar
1 teaspoon baking powder
3 tablespoons melted and
    cooled butter, marga-
    rine or shortening

½ teaspoon salt

Beat egg yolks in large mixing bowl, using electric or hand beater. When thick and fluffy, beat in buttermilk and soda.

Sift together and beat in flour, sugar, baking powder and salt. Beat in butter.

Beat egg whites stiff and fold into mixture.

Bake pancakes on lightly buttered blazer pan until bubbly; turn and bake other side.

BROWN DERBY POTATO PANCAKES
[Serves 8]

2 eggs, well beaten
¼ teaspoon nutmeg
1 teaspoon chopped parsley
3 raw potatoes, grated fine

2 tablespoons flour
½ teaspoon baking powder
Salt
½ cup butter or chicken fat

Beat together eggs, nutmeg, parsley, and potatoes. Add flour, baking powder, and salt to taste. Blend well until smooth. Fry in butter, a tablespoon of batter for each cake. Keep pancakes warm until ready to serve.

MATZO MEAL PANCAKES
[Serves 4]

3 eggs	⅓ teaspoon salt
6 tablespoons milk	¾ cup matzo meal

1½ sticks butter (¾ cup)

Separate eggs; beat yolks, adding cold milk and salt and beating until all is well integrated. Add matzo meal gradually, beating well between additions.

Beat egg whites until stiff but not dry and fold delicately into batter to make it lighter.

Heat butter in blazer pan over medium heat, and drop batter by the tablespoon in hot butter, browning on both sides. Drain on paper towels. Serve with strawberry preserves, jelly or sour cream.

CORNMEAL CAKES
[Makes about 12 pancakes]

1¼ cups buttermilk	½ teaspoon baking soda
1 cup cornmeal	½ teaspoon salt
2 tablespoons flour	1 egg

Put in container of electric blender in order given. Cover and blend on low speed a few seconds.

Spoon onto preheated, well-greased blazer pan. Cook until brown, turning once. Stir batter with spoon each time before baking next batch.

Serve with butter, maple syrup, jelly, jam, preserves or prune or apple butter.

CHEESE BLINTZES
[Makes 18]

2 eggs	orange and lemon peel
1 cup milk	½ cup flour
½ teaspoon salt	3 teaspoons butter
1 teaspoon each, fine-grated	Powdered sugar

Batter: Beat eggs; add milk, salt and grated peel. Pour this into the flour slowly, stirring vigorously for a smooth, thin batter. Butter a blazer pan very slightly; pour in 2 tablespoons of the batter, tilting pan to spread thin over entire bottom of pan. When cooked, the edges will shrink away from sides. Remove pancake to paper or cloth that has been sprinkled with powdered sugar. While cooling, continue to make pancakes, buttering pan slightly between each.

Filling

1½ cups cottage cheese or 1 cup and 1 3-ounce package cream cheese	½ teaspoon ginger
	1 teaspoon vanilla
	2 teaspoons sugar
1 cup sour cream	Butter
1 cup strawberry preserves	

Blend cottage cheese, half the sour cream, ginger, vanilla and sugar. Put 2 tablespoons of filling in the center of each pancake; roll like a jelly roll and place them in shallow pan. Put a dab of butter on top of each; place under broiler or in blazer pan, until heated through.

Serve, three to a portion, topping with remaining sour cream and preserves.

MOCK CHEESE BLINTZES

Cream cheese	Butter
Salted crackers	Currant jelly or strawberry preserves
1 egg to 3 tablespoons milk	

Spread cream cheese between 2 salted crackers. Dip into mixture of egg and milk.

Heat butter in blazer pan; sauté cracker sandwiches on both sides.

Dot with jelly or preserves and serve hot, either as dessert or for tea.

Cheese Dishes and the
Rabbit Habit

Chafing dishes and cheese dishes have been going together since the first Welsh Rabbit, which is alleged to be the oldest cheese dish.

This is how the Welsh Rabbit came about, according to Ancient Legend (an early writer, also known as Aesop Fable):

In Wales, centuries ago, a hunter returned home empty-bagged and told his wife the countryside was bare and bald—not a hare to be found for miles around.

Having heard the cotton-picking tale before, the good wife was ready with a potful of melted cheese and a plate of toasted bread.

"Here's a rabbit for you," she said.

Since she said it in Welsh, the dish has been known as Welsh Rabbit ever since.

Which clearly shows that those of the hoity-toity who insist on calling it a "Rarebit" are a bunch of super-cilliasses.

CHEESE FACTS

One pound of cheese contains the protein and fat of a gallon of whole milk.

To keep cheese, cover with wax paper, then with a piece of cheesecloth well dampened with vinegar. This will stop mold from forming. Don't keep cheese in tightly covered jars.

A FEW WORDS ABOUT
THE COOKING OF CHEESE

In comparison with other food ingredients, cheese is delicate. Too high temperature and too long over heat will overcook cheese so that it is lumpy, stringy and tough. So, use low to moderate heat and cook as short a time as possible. To hasten the cooking process, dice the cheese before adding to the pot; though some recipes call for grating or shredding—which some authorities declare to be not as effective. To keep cheese smooth and tender in a milk sauce, add the diced, grated or shredded cheese to cold milk and heat slowly.

IF YOUR CHEESE RABBIT THICKENS

Thin it down a bit with warm beer (if you've used beer), or milk (if it's non-alcoholic).

In Dr. Sam'l Johnson's time Welsh Rabbit was known as Stewed Cheese and Cheshire was the cheese used, especially at the Cheshire Cheese. It was eaten with tankards of ale as an accompaniment. Ale was not in the recipe in those days, the diners and drinkers figuring that would be too much of a good thing.

Cheshire Cheese is about 500 years older than Cheddar and is the one preferred by the French when making Welsh Rabbits. They call it Chester and season their rabbits with celery salt or seed, or add chopped bits of celery, radish and/or cucumber.

I received the following answer to my inquiry regarding the "meltability" of English cheeses from the English Country Cheese Council:

"Of the English cheese varieties mentioned, Lancashire has the lowest melting point and traditionally is regarded as the finest toasting cheese. In the areas where it is produced it is often referred to as the 'Leigh Toaster.' English Cheshire, too, has long been regarded as an excellent cheese for use in cheese sauces.

"Leicester, Wensleydale, Double Gloucester, Caerphilly and Derby are rather similar when considering 'meltability' but we would recommend Leicester and Wensleydale as crumbly cheeses, Double Gloucester, Derby and Cheddar as close textured grating cheeses particularly when they have been allowed to dry. Caerphilly is very moist and is best used in recipes where sliced cheese is required. An example of this is in the attached Caerphilly cheese recipe for 'Caws Bobi' (Welsh for roasted cheese).

Yours sincerely,
H. R. Cornwell—Cheese Executive"

And from the Council, I received the following three recipes:

BASIC WELSH RABBIT
[Serves 2]

½ pound Lancashire cheese, crumbled	Dash Worcestershire sauce
1 teaspoon dry mustard	Dash paprika
	4 tablespoons milk
4 tablespoons butter	

Place crumbled cheese, mustard, Worcestershire and paprika together in saucepan.

Warm the milk and butter together in another pan until butter melts.

Add milk-butter mixture to cheese mixture and stir and heat until a smooth consistency results.

Spread on toasted white or brown bread and grill until top is golden brown.

Variations: Using basic mixture, add:

Chopped onion	Chopped grilled bacon
Anchovy filets	Mushrooms on top
Onion and cress	Grilled tomatoes on top

RICH RABBIT
[Serves 4]

½ pound Lancashire cheese,   2 eggs
    crumbled   1 egg yolk
5 ounces cream   Salt and pepper to taste

Place all ingredients in saucepan over medium heat and whip until it boils. Serve on hot buttered toast.

There is a traditional tale, often told in Welsh homes over the supper table, of the group of Welshmen who went to heaven and made such a nuisance of themselves that St. Peter was at his wits' end to get rid of them. After much consultation with other angels, he arranged for a cherub to bang and rattle the gates of heaven, shouting "Caws bobi! Caws bobi!" (Roasted cheese!)

With high glee all the Welshmen rushed out to taste their favorite dish—whilst the gates were quickly locked behind them.

CAWS BOBI (Roasted Cheese)
[Serves 5 people or 2 Welshmen]

2 pounds onions, sliced   sliced
    Salt and pepper to taste   1 ounce butter
½ pound Caerphilly cheese,   Paprika

Place onions in a medium baking dish and season. Cover evenly with slices of Caerphilly; dot with bits of butter. Place in 450° oven for 25 to 30 minutes. Before serving, shake a little paprika over the dish.

"The success of your rabbit, as a general rule, depends upon the quality of the cheese used. Poor quality cheese sometimes will make the rabbit stringy instead of smooth and creamy as it should be. Be sure to use a rich, well-aged cheese."—Clara (Mrs. Duncan) Hines.

WELSH RABBIT
[Serves 4]

3 cups grated Cheddar cheese	1 tablespoon Worcestershire sauce
1 teaspoon cornstarch	½ cup beer
1 teaspoon English dry mustard	Salt to taste

In blazer pan mix cheese and cornstarch; add mustard, Worcestershire, beer and salt to taste. Mix well again.

Place on heat and bring to boil, mixing very briskly. When all cheese is melted and the mixture reaches a smooth consistency, serve on toast or English muffins.

Variation 1: Serve Welsh Rabbit over slices of grilled or raw tomatoes instead of toast or hot crackers.

Variation 2: At the seafood restaurant of Gage and Tollner (established 1879 in Brooklyn) they serve a Long Island Rabbit which consists of a regular Welsh Rabbit, heated to bubbling point, then just before serving, the yolk of an egg is dropped in and stirred vigorously.

Offered by someone who said: "Welsh rabbit is frequently at its best when cooked by a French chef."

A SIMPLE FRENCH RABBIT
[Serves 4]

1½ pounds dry Cheddar or Cheshire cheese, in bits	3 drops Worcestershire sauce
Beer	Possibly a pinch of salt
Dash paprika	

Place cheese in top of double boiler over very hot water and stir occasionally with wooden spoon until it melts. As it is melting, gradually add enough beer (stirring now constantly) until you have a thick, smooth sauce. Add Worcestershire, taste before adding salt, and sprinkle paprika over.

Remove from fire. Pour immediately over fresh toasted French bread.

At the Brown Derby restaurants in Hollywood and Beverly Hills, where I committed my first cook book, they serve several dishes that begin with Welsh Rabbit and add other ingredients for Sunday night suppers, luncheons or even light dinners.

RABBIT WITH SHRIMP
[Serves 6]

6 English muffins, split and   12 breaded and fried shrimp
   toasted   3 cups Welsh Rabbit

Place half of muffin on heated plate. Alongside arrange 2 fried shrimp. Cover muffin with rabbit. Cover that with remaining half muffin. Pour over more rabbit. Serve immediately.

RABBIT WITH CHIPPED BEEF
[Serves 6]

6 English muffins, split and   ¼ pound chipped beef,
   toasted   blanched in water
              3 cups Welsh Rabbit

Proceed as with Rabbit with Shrimp above, but instead of shrimp alongside, sprinkle small pieces of chipped beef over all.

RABBIT WITH SMOKED TURKEY
[Serves 6]

6 English muffins, split and   1 cup smoked turkey
   toasted   julienned
              3 cups Welsh Rabbit

Proceed same as for Rabbit with Shrimp, substituting strips of turkey.

This is the way Welsh Rabbit is served at the elegant Hotel Plaza-Athénée in Paris, usually as a luncheon dish.

WELSH RABBIT PLAZA ATHENEE
[Serves 5]

4 egg whites
¼ teaspoon cream of tartar
½ teaspoon baking powder
1 cup Béchamel Sauce (see below)

1½ cups grated Emmentaler cheese
5 slices white toast
Paprika

Beat egg whites with cream of tartar until they form peaks.

Whip ⅓ of whites with baking powder into Béchamel, blending well with wire whip. Fold remaining whites and half the cheese into sauce, gently with a spatula.

Press each slice of toast into a custard cup or ramekin, fitting it into bottom. Fill with mixture and divide remaining cheese over top of the five cups. Sprinkle with paprika and bake in preheated 400° oven until set, 20 to 25 minutes.

BECHAMEL SAUCE NO. 2
[Makes over 1 cup]

3 tablespoons butter
3 tablespoons flour

1 cup milk
Salt and white pepper
Grated nutmeg

Melt butter in saucepan, stir flour in until blended. Add the milk slowly and cook, stirring until sauce is smooth and boiling. Season with salt, pepper and nutmeg. Blend and remove from heat.

And while we're about it, here is another baked cheese dish not dissimilar.

LITTLE CREAM POTS WITH CHEESE
[Serves 6]

4 eggs
2 cups heavy cream
  Salt and cayenne pepper
  to taste
  Pinch nutmeg

1½ cups grated Gruyère
  cheese
3 rashers cooked, crumbled
  bacon

Beat eggs and gradually add cream, then salt, cayenne and nutmeg. Add 1 cup of the cheese and stir well.

Divide among 6 *pot de crème* cups or ramekins; divide crumbled bacon over tops.

Place cups in pan of hot water and bake in preheated 350° oven until set, about 30 minutes. Remaining cheese may be sprinkled over tops 5 minutes before taking cups out, or just before serving. Serve hot or cold.

A.1. WELSH RABBIT
[Serves 6]

4 tablespoons butter
4 tablespoons flour
2 cups milk or light cream

1 tablespoon A.1. sauce
2 teaspoons prepared mustard
1 teaspoon salt

1 cup grated strong cheese

In blazer pan over low heat melt butter; blend in flour; add milk; stir with wire whisk until thick and smooth. Add A.1. sauce, mustard and salt, blending well. Drop in cheese a little at a time, melting each batch before adding next. Heat well.

Serve on buttered toast or toasted crackers with broiled tomato halves or thick slices.

GREEN PEA RABBIT
[Serves 4]

1½ cups tender green peas, cooked
2 tablespoons butter
¾ cup diced Colby or Cheddar cheese
1 teaspoon salt
1 teaspoon Worcestershire or soy sauce
¼ teaspoon paprika
1 cup milk

Mash peas or put through blender until pureed.

Melt butter in blazer pan and slowly add cheese, stirring until melted.

Add peas, salt, Worcestershire and paprika and stir until mixture is creamy. Then add milk slowly and stir while cooking until mixture is as thick as desired.

Variation:

Boston Rabbit: Substitute for green peas 1 cup pureed or mashed baked beans with tomato sauce.

Next, a number of melted cheese dishes with ingredients from and names of various other countries in the spirit of Welsh Rabbit. The first two are traditional, but the dozen that follow are mostly my own creation.

ENGLISH MONKEY
[Serves 4]

1 cup dry breadcrumbs
1 cup milk
1 tablespoon butter
1 cup English cheese (Double Gloucester, Cheddar, Cheshire, Lancashire), diced
1 egg, lightly beaten
½ teaspoon salt
1 grind fresh pepper
Dash cayenne

Soak breadcrumbs in milk 15 minutes.

Melt butter in blazer pan over water; add cheese and let melt with minimum stirring. Then add moistened breadcrumbs, egg, salt, pepper and cayenne. When blended, cook 3 minutes longer, then pour over toasted English muffins or crackers.

SCOTCH WOODCOCK
[Serves 8]

1 large (28-ounce) can
  tomatoes
¾ pound Dunlop, Cheddar or
  American cheese, in bits

3 eggs, beaten
Salt and fresh-ground
  pepper, to taste
Sprinkle cayenne

Well-toasted crackers

Put tomatoes in blazer pan over direct heat and, when bubbling, add cheese and stir until melted.

Place pan over boiling water and add eggs, cooking and stirring until just thickened. Season to taste and sprinkle cayenne over. Serve immediately on crackers.

IRISH O'HAIRE
[Serves 4]

1 8-ounce package cream
  cheese
1 pound Blarney (or
  Cheddar) cheese,
  shredded
½ cup Guinness stout

Sprinkle onion salt
¼ teaspoon dry mustard
Dash Tabasco sauce
6 slices Irish (if available)
  bacon, cooked crisp and
  crumbled

Melt cream cheese slowly over direct heat in blazer pan, stirring constantly. Add other cheese, stout and seasonings, stirring constantly while cooking until cheese is melted. Add bacon and keep warm over hot water, unless serving immediately. If it becomes too thick, add a bit of milk.

Serve over toasted Irish bread or soda bread.

You know about Bombay Duck, a small dried fish that accompanies curry. Well, here's a dish where the bird has flown away before the cooking starts.

DUTCH DUCK
[Serves 4]

4 tablespoons butter
4 tablespoons flour
2 cups milk
1 teaspoon Worcestershire
   sauce
Dash Tabasco sauce
2 cups shredded Edam or
   Gouda cheese
2 cups cooked rice
1 teaspoon curry powder
3 tablespoons soft butter

Heat butter in blazer pan over medium heat; add flour and stir until bubbling.

Set pan over hot water. Stir in milk and cook until thickened, stirring every once in a while. Add Worcestershire, Tabasco and cheese, a handful at a time. Stir with wooden spoon until cheese melts.

Either add rice, curry and butter and heat well; or place hot rice in serving dish, blend in butter and curry and pour cheese mixture over.

Serve on heated plates.

A quick, simple recipe:

BELGIAN BUNNY
[Serves 4]

1 can condensed Cheddar
   cheese soup
1 can condensed tomato soup
1 cup beer (or water)
1 teaspoon caraway seeds
1 teaspoon dry mustard
1 teaspoon Worcestershire
   sauce
Toast triangles

In chafing dish blazer pan over water blend soups, beer and seasonings and heat until bubbling, stirring with wooden spoon until smooth. Do not boil.

Serve over toast in heated plates.

Androuët, the "maître fromager" or cheese-master of Paris, lists around 250 different French cheeses for sale at his store on the rue d'Amsterdam. Phil Alpert of Cheeses of All Nations on Chambers Street in Manhattan has 386, from Aiguilles to Vocel. Of these, any of the following can be used in the following recipe: Fondue Fromage, Fondue Cancoillotte, Fontina, Gourmandaise, Gruyère, Noisette de Gruyère, or Gouda Français.

FRENCH COW
[Serves 4]

½ cup Chablis or Graves (dry white wine)
1 teaspoon Dijon (hot) mustard
1 pound French cheese (see above), shredded
1 cup minced mushrooms
Pinch cayenne pepper
Salt and pepper to taste
2 eggs, well beaten

In blazer pan heat wine and mustard together, mixing well. Add cheese by handfuls and stir with wooden spoon; add mushrooms and seasonings. Cook until smooth, about 15 minutes. Add eggs, mix well and serve at once on crusty or toasted French bread.

ITALIAN PEASANT PHEASANT
[Serves 4]

3 tablespoons butter
1 large can tomatoes
1 cup grated Parmesan cheese
1 large green pepper, chopped
1 small onion, grated
4 eggs, well beaten
1½ teaspoons salt

Melt butter in blazer pan over direct heat.
Mix tomatoes, cheese, pepper and grated onion.
Transfer blazer pan to over water pan; add mixture and heat well. Add eggs and salt, cook until eggs are creamy, stirring and scraping from bottom of pan.
Serve on toasted Italian bread.

If you can get Salami Raucher (an Austrian cheese like Gouda, lightly smoked and with chunks of salami), use a pound, diced. Otherwise use ¾ pound of the cheeses named and ¼ pound cut-up salami.

VIENNESE VENISON
[Serves 4]

1 tablespoon butter
1 tablespoon flour
¼ teaspoon cayenne
¼ teaspoon salt
1 pound Salami Raucher, or ¾ pound Alpinekäse,

Schachtelkäse or Gruyère and ¼ pound salami, all diced
2 eggs
½ tablespoon Worcestershire sauce
1 cup dry white wine

Melt butter in blazer pan over hot water.

Mix flour, cayenne and salt together. Add to melted butter and stir. Add diced cheese and salami gradually until cheese begins to melt.

Warm wine slightly in separate pot and add to pan, stirring in thoroughly.

Beat eggs well, add Worcestershire to them, then gradually stir this into pan mixture and cook until smooth and salami bits are well distributed.

Serve on thin toast or crisp crackers.

SWISS CHAMOIS
[Serves 6]

½ cup flour
2 teaspoons dry mustard
2 tablespoons Worcestershire sauce
Dash Tabasco sauce
3 cups milk
6 slices bread
2 tablespoons soft butter

1 tablespoon fine-chopped watercress
½ cup butter
2 cups grated Emmentaler cheese
1 cup grated Gruyère cheese
1 cup shredded dried beef (or prosciutto)

Blend flour and mustard.

Add Worcestershire and Tabasco to milk.

Toast bread and spread with soft butter mixed with watercress.

Heat ½ cup butter in blazer pan over flame until it

sizzles; blend in flour and mustard. Stir in milk gradually and cheeses by handful until mixture thickens and cheese melts. Add beef, stir well and heat 5 minutes longer.

Serve on the toast on heated plates.

RUSSIAN ROE
[Serves 4]

1 8-ounce package cream cheese
4 tablespoons Russian dressing
1 teaspoon prepared mustard
1 teaspoon grated onion
Dash garlic or seasoned salt
3 tablespoons dry white wine
1 small jar black or red caviar

Melt cream cheese slowly in chafing dish over direct heat, stirring constantly. Blend in dressing, mustard, onion and salt until well heated. Add wine and keep heated over hot water. Just before serving over toast, mix in caviar or divide it over 4 servings as topping.

In the spirit of Welsh Rabbit, here is a fake crab dish.

CANADIAN CRAB
[Serves 4]

2 tablespoons butter
3/4 pound Canadian Cheddar or Colby cheese, in small bits
1 1/2 tablespoons anchovy
paste
2/3 teaspoon salt
2/3 teaspoon dry mustard
Sprinkle cayenne pepper
3 egg yolks
3/4 cup cream

Melt butter in blazer pan over hot water. Add cheese, anchovy paste and seasonings.

Stir egg yolks into cream and blend.

When mixture in pan has melted and blended, add cream and egg mixture; stir continually until smooth. Serve immediately on toasted bread or crackers.

MONTEREY JACKRABBIT
[Serves 4]

3 tablespoons butter
⅓ cup minced green pepper
⅓ cup minced celery
3 ounces diced fresh (or
    canned and drained)
    mushrooms
5 tablespoons all-purpose
    flour

1 tablespoon prepared
    mustard
1 teaspoon Worcestershire
    sauce
1 cup beer or milk
1 pound Monterey Jack
    cheese, shredded
Toasted sourdough bread

Melt butter in blazer pan over direct heat; add pepper, celery and mushrooms. Cook until tender; remove from heat.

Blend in flour, mustard and Worcestershire. Add beer or milk all at once.

Return to heat and cook, stirring until thickened. Add cheese a handful at a time, cooking and stirring until cheese melts. If too thick, thin a bit with more beer or milk.

Keep mixture warm over hot water. Serve over sourdough bread that has been toasted and (optional) spread with garlic butter.

This recipe is from Mrs. James English of Beverly Hills.

MEXICAN ROAD-RUNNER
[Serves 4]

3 tablespoons butter
1 small onion, fine-chopped
2 tablespoons flour
1 cup milk
2 cups grated sharp
    Cheddar cheese
1½ cups stewed tomatoes

1 small can chili peppers,
    chopped
1 teaspoon salt
⅛ teaspoon fresh-ground
    pepper
1 teaspoon Worcestershire
    sauce
2 egg yolks, well beaten

Melt butter in blazer pan of chafing dish over low heat. Add onion and sauté until transparent.

Place pan over water, add flour and blend well; add

milk gradually, stirring constantly until thick and smooth. Stir in cheese. When melted, add tomatoes, chilies, salt, pepper and Worcestershire. Cook 10 minutes over low heat, then blend in egg yolks. Continue to cook 3 to 4 minutes.

Serve over tortillas, tostados or Holland rusk rounds on heated plates.

PINK POODLE
[Serves 6]

1 tablespoon minced onion
3 tablespoons butter
1 tablespoon flour
2 tablespoons claret, or other dry wine
1 can cream of tomato soup

½ teaspoon salt
¼ teaspoon pepper
Dash of powdered clove
¾ pound sharp cheese, cut in small pieces
1 pinch soda

1 egg slightly beaten

In blazer pan cook onion in butter till soft and yellow. Add flour and, when well blended, the claret and tomato soup. Stir in the seasonings, then the cheese, stirring till the cheese is melted. Add the soda, then the egg slightly beaten. Stir till very smooth.

Serve on thin hot toast with more of the claret on the side.

PICKLED RABBIT
[Serves 4]

2 tablespoons butter or margarine
1 tablespoon all-purpose flour
1 cup milk
2 cups grated Cheddar cheese (about ½ pound)

2 teaspoons prepared mustard
⅓ cup chopped sweet gherkins
Salt and pepper to taste
Tomato wedges
Toast

Melt butter (or margarine) and blend in flour. Gradually add milk and cook over low heat, stirring constantly, until thickened. Add cheese, mustard and gherkins. Cook, stirring constantly, until cheese is all melted. Season with salt and pepper. Serve over tomato wedges and toast.

RAT-TRAP RABBIT
[Serves 3]

½ pound rat-trap (American Cheddar) cheese
3 tablespoons butter
2 teaspoons Worcestershire sauce
2 teaspoons dry mustard
4 tablespoons cream
2 eggs
6 slices toast
Paprika

Chop or grate or cut cheese into same-size pieces.

Melt butter in blazer pan over hot water. Add cheese, Worcestershire, mustard and cream, but do not stir. Rake contents gently and mix well by poking until cheese is all melted. Remove from heat and add eggs, beating lightly. Heat of cheese will cook egg. Pour over toast in individual serving dishes and sprinkle with touch of paprika.

Instead of cream, milk, evaporated milk, beer or dry white wine can be used.

PEPPY RABBIT
[Serves 6]

3 cups (¾ pound) shredded Cheddar cheese
1¼ cups milk
1 egg, beaten
2 tablespoons minced pimiento
1 teaspoon Worcestershire sauce
¾ teaspoon dry mustard
1 dash Tabasco sauce

Combine all ingredients except pimiento in blazer pan; cook over hot water, stirring constantly, until cheese is melted and rabbit is slightly thickened. Stir in pimiento and serve immediately over toast points, toasted muffins or cooked mushroom caps.

Here is the recipe for a chafing dish rabbit given to me by Arno Schmidt, the executive chef of the Waldorf-Astoria Hotel in New York City.

WALDORF-ASTORIA RABBIT
[Serves 4 to 6]

2 tablespoons butter	sauce
1 pound mellow American	Salt to taste
cheese, in small pieces	Dash cayenne
1 tablespoon dry mustard	1 cup light beer
½ teaspoon Worcestershire	1 egg

Melt butter in blazer pan of chafing dish; add cheese and melt very slowly.

Meanwhile, mix mustard, Worcestershire, salt and cayenne with 1 tablespoon of the beer. Add egg and beat together. Set aside.

As the cheese melts, add the remainder of the beer slowly, stopping when the consistency of the mixture is like thick cream, stirring constantly in the same direction. The melting and stirring-in of the beer should take at least 30 minutes. Be careful that it never bubbles.

When perfectly smooth, stir in the egg and seasonings. The cheese mixture should be hot enough so that the egg thickens it slightly.

Pour over toasted bread on very hot plates.

What to do during the 30 minutes? Easy. Have the guests take turns stirring.

Equally good in chafing dish, at a barbecue fire or during a camp-out, is

EASY RABBIT
[Serves 6]

1 tablespoon butter or	¾ pound shredded Cheddar
margarine	cheese
1½ tablespoons chopped	¾ teaspoon salt
onion	1 egg
1 medium can tomato soup	2 tablespoons cold water
6 slices toasted bread	

In pan or skillet, brown onion in melted butter; stir in soup; add cheese gradually, and salt, stirring until cheese is melted and smooth (about 10 minutes).

Beat egg with water. Add slowly to cheese and tomato mixture.

Serve hot on the toast.

If you are addicted to the Late Show, you are familiar with the clean-cut, square-cut face of Richard Arlen, who has changed remarkably little over the years. Here is a favorite recipe of his from the old Hollywood days.

SPAGHETTI RABBIT A L'ARLEN
[Serves 4]

1 8-ounce package spaghetti	American cheese
1½ tablespoons butter	2 eggs, well beaten
1½ tablespoons flour	1 tablespoon catsup
¼ teaspoon dry mustard	1 teaspoon Worcestershire
½ teaspoon salt	sauce
1 cup milk	1 tomato, sliced
½ pound sharp Cheddar or	1 green pepper in rings

Cook spaghetti in boiling salted water for 8 minutes; drain; set aside on heated platter.

In blazer pan over medium heat, melt butter; add flour, mustard and salt and cook 3 or 4 minutes. Add milk and cheese and cook, stirring constantly, until cheese is melted and sauce has thickened.

Stir several tablespoons of sauce into the eggs, then pour this into sauce. Add catsup and Worcestershire and cook, stirring constantly, for 1 minute.

Pour sauce over spaghetti in heated platter. Garnish with tomato slices and pepper rings and serve immediately.

SUNBEAM WELSH RABBIT
[Serves 4 to 6]

½ cup flour

½ teaspoon salt

Dash seasoned salt

Dash cayenne pepper

¼ teaspoon dry mustard

¼ teaspoon celery seed

2 cups cream

½ pound sharp natural American cheese, sliced

½ teaspoon Worcestershire sauce

¼ cup butter

1 cup additional cream

Combine all ingredients except butter and additional cream in blender container. Cover, blend on low speed for ½ minute, stopping to scrape down.

Pour into blazer pan. Add butter and additional cream. Cook, stirring, over medium heat until thickened.

Serve over rye or white toast.

A DIRECTORY OF CHEESES
FOR CHAFING DISHES

Here are most of the cheeses you can buy in the United States for making cheese chafing dishes. They were selected for their meltability and availability.

While a number may be difficult to find in the limited cases of grocery and dairy stores, almost all can be purchased in cheese specialty shops—and all are available at such emporia as Cheeses of All Nations, 153 Chambers Street, New York, N.Y. 10007; Cheese Village, 3 Greenwich Avenue, New York, N.Y. 10014; and Cheese Unlimited, 1263 Lexington Ave., New York, N.Y. 10028. These three establishments do a mail order business to anywhere in continental United States.

Large department stores with food departments (such as Macy's and Bloomingdale's in Manhattan) also have extensive selections of cheeses. So does William Poll, 1051 Lexington Ave.

ALPINEKÄSE: From Austria, mellow, firm, Swiss family.

AMERICAN: Same as Cheddar. Comes "natural," "processed," "processed cheese food" and "spread." Only the natural is recommended, as the others contain fillers, chemicals, etc. which interfere with the melting process, with the result that the "cheese" becomes stringy, like plastic, or refuses to melt. A great many American eaters know of no other cheese but this manufactured and manipulated gunk, mainly because it comes in convenient sandwich-slice form and, due to addition of preservatives, it keeps well.

APPENZELLER: A Swiss manufactured in Canton of Appenzell, made usually from skimmed cow's milk, sometimes whole; soaked in cider or white wine and spices. Zesty, nut-like.

APPLE CHEESE: A lightly smoked American cheese.

ASADERO: Also called Oaxaca, white, whole-milk Mexican. Melts easily. Asadero: "fit for roasting." Originated in state of Oaxaca, now mostly made in Jalisco.

ASIAGO: Originated in town of that name in Vicenza, Italy. From cow's milk. Hard, zesty, grated and mixed with other cheeses, or sprinkled like Parmesan.

AUSTRALIAN RAW MILK CHEDDAR: Natural, pale, mellow cheese good for cooking.

AUSTRIAN PURBON: Firm, zesty, good keeper, from Austrian Alps, grills well.

BAMBINO: A delicate cheese from Italy which is sweet and mild. Recommended for children.

BATTELMATT: Nutty, sharp Swiss, made in Canton of Tessin; softer and moister than Emmentaler.

BEAUFORT: Cow's milk; nutty, harder than Gruyère, from Savoie.

BEL PAESE: "Beautiful country." Trade name of popular Italian table cheese. Soft, sweet, mild, smooth, mellow. Usually a dessert cheese, but can be combined with other, harder cheeses for melting. Map on label tells you if it is made in Italy or is domestic.

BITTO: Italian, from Lombardy; firm Swiss-type; similar to Fontina and Montasio, from cow's milk, mixture cow's and goat, or ewe's milk, skimmed or whole. Nutty, zesty, best grated for melting.

BLARNEY: Ireland's answer to Emmentaler, but a faint echo.

CAERPHILLY: Made and popular in Wales; semi-soft, cow's milk; white, smooth, granular.

CANTAL (also known locally as FOURME): A hard, yellow

cheese with piquant flavor and firm, close body. Made for centuries in region of Auvergne Mountains, Dept. of Cantal, France. The French cheese that most resembles Cheddar. But since it varies in flavor, taste before buying.

CHEDDAR: Originally made in Somersetshire village of Cheddar; first cheese factory in U.S. was Jesse Williams' in 1851 at Rome, N.Y. About 1½ billion pounds now made annually in U.S., making it by far the most popular. Also known as American and American Cheddar. Variations include Black Diamond Cheddar, Cherry Hill Cheddar, Smoked Cheddar, Cheddar Français, Irish, Australian, Canadian, Canadian Cheddar and Rum, Port Wine Cheddar Spread, Czechoslovakian, English Farmhouse, Minor Aged, New Zealand, Queso de Papa (Puerto Rico), Scottish; and from U.S.: California, Daisy, Illinois mellow and sharp, Kentucky mellow and sharp, Minnesota mellow, Minnesota Sharpy, Natural Longhorn, New England Rat Cheese, Atomic from Ohio, sharp; Ohio State mellow, Rocky Mountain Blacky, Young American, Wisconsin Longhorn, medium sharp, sharp.

CHESHIRE: Also called Chester, first made at village of Chester on River Dee; said to have been originally molded in shape of famous Cheshire Cat. Like Cheddar, but more crumbly; mellow, smooth, semi-hard.

CHEVROTIN: Goat's milk cheese from Savoie.

COLBY: Similar to Cheddar; made in Australia, Belgium, New Zealand, Scotland and Sweden, in addition to U.S. Has softer body and more moisture than Cheddar. One of the cheeses the author enjoys the most.

COMTÉ: Made in Franche-Comté, Jura Mountains of eastern France, resembles Gruyère, with little holes.

COON: A Cheddar cured by a special patented method; dark rind, white inside; crumbly, with sharp, tangy flavor.

CORNHUSKER: Introduced in Nebraska over 30 years ago. Similar to Cheddar and Colby, but softer and moister. A "rat-trap" cheese.

DANBO, DANISH EXPORT: Plain and seeded with caraway; mellow, made with skim milk and buttermilk; shaped like Gouda.

DERBY: Made in Derbyshire from cow's whole milk; similar to Cheddar but more flaky and moister; zesty and firm when it matures. SAGE DERBY with sage leaves.

DORSET: Semi-hard, use grated; zesty and smooth, blend a little with Cheddar to add flavor; blue-veined.

DUNLOP: Rich, white, made in Scotland; resembles Cheddar.

EDAM: The mild, mellow, younger type can be cooked. Dutch, imported, but also made in U.S. Between 8 and 9 pounds of cheese is obtained from 100 pounds of milk.

EMMENTALER: Named after Emme Valley, Canton of Bern, where it originated. This is what is usually sold as Swiss cheese. Has large holes or eyes, because it "rises" similarly to bread; has hazel nut or walnut flavor and ripe, strong smell when aged, though wheels imported to U.S. are mild. But 80 years ago at U.S. free lunch counters it exuded most pungent aroma. Made here in Wisconsin and Ohio, quite good; brought in from Finland and sold as "Imported Swiss," but no word as to country of origin; a mild Emmentaler comes from Austria and Blarney from Ireland is just that. Samsoë is the Danish version.

ESTROM: Rich, soft Danish, Port Salut type. Very pleasing.

FLANDERS: A mellow Gouda type, from Belgium.

FONDUTTA: A fatter, softer version of Muenster, made in Wisconsin.

FONTINA: A great Italian cheese, made of ewe's milk in the Aosta Valley of Piedmont.

FORMAGGIO DI CAPRA: Mild, smooth Italian goat cheese.

FYNBO: A rich cheese of the Samsoë family and Samsoë is the Danish Gruyère.

GERÔME (also known as GERARDMER): From Lorraine and nearby Switzerland. Soft, creamy, greenish tint.

DOUBLE GLOUCESTER: Similar to Cheddar but has slightly pungent flavor. Smooth velvet texture and beautiful golden color.

GOLD 'N' RICH: A bland American cheese halfway between Bel Paese and Muenster in flavor. Melts and cooks well.

GOUDA, PLAIN and SMOKED: Has more fat than Edam.

GOUDA WITH KÜMMEL SEEDS: Flavored with light Burgundy wine. A blended cheese which can be used in combination with others.

GOURMANDAISE: Mellow white French cheese flavored with kirsch.

GOYA: An Argentine cheese, nutty, delicate, firm and tasty.

GRUYÈRE (also known as GROYER and VACHELIN): Named for village of Gruyère, Canton of Fribourg, Switzerland. With Emmentaler, the most important Swiss cheese. Is darker, nuttier, sharper, and has smaller holes than Emmentaler.

CRÈME DE GRUYÈRE: A soft, smooth Gruyère made in France.

NOISETTE DE GRUYÈRE: A smooth, delicate Gruyère made with nuts in France.

GRUYÈRE WITH PISTACHIOS: A blended cheese made in New York, perfumed with Neufchâtel wine.

HAVARTI and HAVARTI SEEDED: Light yellow Danish cheese with distinctive flavor and numerous holes. Use fairly fresh. The seeded comes with caraway.

HERKIMER COUNTY: A Cheddar-type cheese made in New York State. Fairly dry and crumbly, with sharp flavor.

HICKORY SMOKED: One of the Cheddars made in the U.S. Hard.

ISRAEL TABLE CHEESE: A new, special product created by modern methods.

JARLSBERG: Norway's answer to Swiss. Nutty, delicate flavor; wide-eyed, well-textured, buttery.

DOMESTIC KASSERI: Tastes somewhere between Parmesan and Cheddar.

KUMINOST: Spiced with cumin and caraway seed, made from skim milk in Scandinavian countries.

LA MOTHE: A mellow goat cheese from Poitou.

LANCASHIRE, PLAIN and SAGE: Very good melting and toasting version of Cheddar made in Lancaster, England.

LEYDEN: Mellow, spiced Dutch cheese; will add a certain kick when blended with other cheese. DELFT is almost exactly the same.

LONGHORN: Made in Texas, Michigan, Wisconsin and now Minnesota; zesty, old-fashioned Cheddar.

MARIBO: An unusual Danish cheese with a haunting aftertaste; semi-hard, smooth, zesty.

MAY: Made in U.S., mellow, soft Gouda type.

MICHIGAN PINCONICK: A sharp Cheddar.

MIMOLETTE: French, firm, yellow, sharp.

MONTASIO: A hard Italian cheese, to be grated like Parmesan.

MONTEREY JACK: A California cheese made from goat's milk, somewhat like Muenster but not so bland, with small holes. Excellent for melting.

MOUNTAIN: A new Gruyère type from Israel.

MOZZARELLA: Best known as the pizza cheese. Care must be taken in cooking to keep it from going stringy.

MUENSTER or MÜNSTER: Made in Germany, France, Denmark, Switzerland, Norway and the U.S. A pleasing, semi-soft, bland cheese. Comes also with caraway seeds.

MUENSTER WALNUT SPREAD: Blended cheese made in New York, with nuts and perfumed with Chablis.

MUTSCHLI: A Swiss goat's milk cheese.

MYSOST: A mild, sweet Norwegian cheese.

NEW ENGLAND RAT: A sharp Cheddar.

NEW YORK STATE CHEDDAR: Both medium and medium-sharp Cheddars.

NEW YORK STATE CHEDDAR WITH CASHEWS: A blended cheese spread, with nuts and perfumed with white wine.

ONION: A firm cheese with onions for those who like onion flavor in their chafing dishes.

PARMESAN: The classic Italian hard, grating cheese. Adds a zesty touch to cheese chafing dishes if mixed with other cheeses.

PEPPER and HOT PEPPER: Firm, spicy, peppery American cheeses.

PFISTER: Although made differently, classed in the same group with Swiss cheeses.

PINEAPPLE: Gets its name from its shape and color and surface, but it is a well-cured Cheddar type cheese. Mellow.

PROVOLONE: Made all over Italy and in Wisconsin and Michigan. Mellow, smooth, white. Blend with a Swiss for cheese dishes.

PROVOLONE WITH CHIANTI: A blended cheese spread made in New York City; melts easily.

PUMPKIN: Named for shape and color; sharp, dry, firm; between Cheddar and Muenster.

RACLETTE BAGNE: The scraping cheese used in making Raclette, the Swiss melted cheese dish. Also for table use and for fondues. From the Valais region of Switzerland.

REBLOCHON: Strong, smelly, soft, French, buttery, occasionally used for chafing dishes.

REGGIANO: Similar to Parmesan and used in the same manner.

SAGE: An American cheese of the Cheddar family spiced with the herb.

SALAMI RAUCHER: Austrian version of Gouda, lightly smoked, with chunks of salami. Also made with ham.

SAMSOË: Danish version of Swiss Emmentaler.

SAPSAGO: Small, hard cheese from Switzerland with powdered clover leaves. Used grated and in that form an unusual addition to cheese dishes.

SARDO: A hard Italian grating cheese used like Parmesan.

SCHACHTELKÄSE: Made in Austria, Muenster type, sharp and zesty.

SWISS: The over-all name for Emmentaler, made in Switzerland and exported as "Switzerland Swiss." Copies are made in the U.S., France, Denmark, Germany, Italy, Austria, Finland, Russia, and Argentina.

TALEGGIO: A delicious cheese from Italy, often used for dessert.

TILLAMOOK: A tasty Cheddar made in the Pacific Northwest and Colorado.

TILSITER: A North German and Central European soft, smelly cheese with a distinctive taste, sometimes spiced with caraway seeds.

TURUNMAÄ: A mild pasteurized milk cheese imported from Finland, much like California Monterey Jack.

TYBO: Partly skim milk, like Edam, made in Denmark; also comes caraway seeded.

VACHERIN FONDUE: Made in Switzerland much the same as Swiss. After it is cured, it is melted and spices added.

VALIO GRUYÈRE: A firm, mellow Finnish version.

VERITABLE ST. MORITZ: Semi-firm Switzerland cheese, Canton of Graubijenden. Pungent, multi-useful.

VERMONT MAPLE and VERMONT SAGE: Cheddar cheeses

made in that state with the addition of maple flavoring or sage herb.

WARWICKSHIRE: An English cheese very similar to Derby.

WENSLEYDALE: Creamy Yorkshire cheese with subtle flavor, flaky texture and pale parchment color.

WILTSHIRE: Another English cheese similar to Derby; Cheddar family.

WISCONSIN TOP HAT: An American Cheddar, usually aged and sharp.

The apricot-yellow color of the Cheddars, Cheshires and American cheeses are not natural, but due to the addition of annatto, a harmless vegetable dye. Before it was discovered, 200 years ago, all sorts of other dyes were tried, some toxic and others adding an undesirable taste. The leaves of wild pot marigold, carrot juice, saffron and even common household dyes were tried.

And in those bad old days, unscrupulous grocers bored holes in ordinary pale cheese and sold it as "Swiss"!

ON COOKING FISH

Seafood and fish are ideal candidates for chafing dish cookery because of the time element. They should not be overcooked—just enough to coagulate the protein. Longer cooking only toughens the flesh. It also bores the onlookers.

Seafood and the Sad Story of Ben Wenberg

Think chafing dish and you think Lobster Newberg.

The evolution of this dish may be new to you. That is, if you haven't read my chapter on the Delmonico restaurants and their influence on American cuisine in *The American Heritage Cook Book*.

A New York shipping man named Ben Wenberg returned home from a South American trip with a new way to prepare lobster. He imparted the method to the chefs at his favorite eatery, the stylish Delmonico restaurant, the foremost one in the U.S. They whipped it up for him and he always added a bit of secret ingredient which he carried about in a little silver tube. This proved to be paprika, a relatively unknown spice in America in those days.

Friends of Mr. Wenberg and other Delmonico patrons liked the dish so much it was put on the menu as Lobster Wenberg and the author of the specialty enjoyed a certain celebrity for a while.

Alas, he ran afoul of the one inflexible rule of the restaurant—he got into a fist fight there. And so he was barred. Not only that, but Charles Delmonico ordered his name removed from his favorite dish. (It must have been a helluva fight.) What to call it? Simple. Just switch the first three letters around. Lobster Wenberg became Lobster Newberg. And not Newburg, if you want to be authentic.

LOBSTER NEWBERG (né Wenberg)
[Serves 4]

4 ounces (1 stick) butter
3 cups cooked lobster meat, in large chunks
6 egg yolks, lightly beaten with 1 tablespoon light cream

Salt and cayenne to taste
1 pint heavy cream
½ cup Madeira or sherry

Heat butter in blazer pan; add lobster and salt and cayenne. Cook 5 minutes. Pour in cream and bring just to a boil; add wine. Remove from flame, stir 1 tablespoon of mixture into egg yolks and blend well, then add this to mixture and cook over boiling water until heated and thickened, stirring continuously. Do not allow to boil.

Spoon pieces of lobster either into patty shells, over rice or on toast, on heated plates, and pour sauce over.

With lobster meat selling for $6 a pound, *wholesale,* this is called

MILLIONAIRE'S CHAFING DISH
[Serves 4]

2 tablespoons butter
2 truffles, chopped
3 egg yolks
1 cup heavy cream

1 pound cooked lobster meat, in 1-inch pieces
Salt and cayenne pepper
Paprika

Sherry

Melt butter in blazer pan of chafing dish over boiling water or medium direct heat. Add truffles, egg yolks mixed with the cream, and lobster meat.

Stir constantly and cook until well thickened. Season to taste with salt, cayenne and paprika. Add sherry to taste and serve over toast, crackers or in patty shells.

Hines and Smart perfected the package which enables lobsters to be flown anywhere in the U.S. from their headquarters in Boston and still arrive live and pinching.

H & S LOBSTER STEW
[Serves 4]

4 ounces (one stick) butter
12 ounces (1⅔ to 2 cups) cooked lobster meat
½ pint sherry
Salt and fresh-ground pepper

Pinch paprika
1 pint heavy cream
1 pint milk
1 tablespoon butter

Melt butter in blazer pan; add lobster meat and sauté until golden. Add sherry, salt and pepper to taste and paprika and cook over low heat 5 minutes.

Add cream and milk, increase heat and let come just to boil. Remove from heat, add butter and serve at once.

The following is the Luchow recipe for Curry of Lobster, adapted for home use.

CURRY OF LOBSTER LUCHOW
[Serves 4 to 6]

3 1½-pound lobsters
Butter
3 stalks celery, sliced
1 large onion, sliced
1 leek, sliced
3 sprigs parsley
1 clove garlic, crushed
1 bay leaf
1 teaspoon dried thyme

4 tablespoons flour
4 tablespoons curry powder
2 green apples, peeled, cored and sliced
1 tablespoon tomato puree
½ cup shredded coconut
1 teaspoon salt
¼ teaspoon sugar
¼ cup heavy cream

Lobster and sauce are prepared ahead of time, even night before.

Cook lobsters in boiling salted water to cover well for 15 minutes. Allow to cool in cooking liquid, then remove, reserving liquid. Take meat from shells and cut in 1-inch pieces.

Make sauce by melting 2 tablespoons butter in large saucepan. Add celery, onion, leek, parsley, garlic, bay leaf and thyme. Cook over low heat, stirring frequently until mixture is golden brown. Stir in flour, curry powder, apple slices, tomato puree, coconut, salt, sugar and 4 cups of the lobster cooking liquid. Bring to a boil. Reduce heat and simmer over medium heat, stirring occasionally, 1 hour. Strain or force through food mill.

When ready to serve, heat sauce through in blazer pan, then add lobster meat and cook 4 minutes longer. Remove from heat, stir in cream and serve with more coconut sprinkled over top.

Serve with pilaf of rice and chutney.

The lovely and talented ballerina and film star, Tamara Toumanova, is also a creative cook, as witness the following.

TOUMANOVA'S CHAFING DISH
[Serves 6]

4 tablespoons butter
½ pound whole, stemmed, medium-size mushroom caps, preferably fresh
2 cups cooked crabmeat and 1 cup cooked shrimp (or 3 cups shrimp)
½ cup cognac
½ teaspoon sugar
1 cup heavy cream
1 package frozen peas, defrosted
2 egg yolks, beaten
Salt to taste
¼ teaspoon cayenne
1 tablespoon chopped fresh dill (or parsley)

Heat butter in blazer pan and sauté mushroom caps 6 minutes or less. Do not overcook. Add seafood and cognac and cook together 2 minutes more. Add cream and peas and cook another 2 minutes. Add egg yolks, salt, cayenne, dill and sugar and mix very well. Stir and cook until thickened and heated through.

May be served on toasted muffins, plain toast, rice or noodles.

How can she eat such rich dishes and retain her sensational figure? She dances.

SEAFOOD NEWBERG
[Serves 6]

6 tablespoons butter or margarine	1 teaspoon salt
3 cups cut-up lobster, crabmeat, shrimp and/or scallops	1/8 teaspoon paprika
	3 tablespoons sherry
	1/4 teaspoon Tabasco sauce
	1 cup light cream
2 tablespoons flour	1 cup milk

2 eggs yolks, beaten

Melt butter in blazer pan directly over flame. Add seafood and cook, stirring occasionally until it is heated. Sprinkle in flour, salt and paprika over seafood; mix in sherry.

Place over hot water pan. Gradually add Tabasco, light cream, milk and egg yolks. Cook, stirring constantly, until mixture is thickened.

Serve on rice or toast triangles.

Variations: All lobster meat makes it Lobster Newberg, etc.

In back of the American Embassy in Rome, at 7 Via Marche, you'll find George's, a pleasant "Englishman's epicure version of a fine Italian restaurant."

DEVILED SEA FRUIT ALLA GEORGE
[Serves 4]

2 pounds sea fruits (clams, mussels, etc.) weighed in shells

2 pounds jumbo shrimp, weighed in shells

1 pound baby shrimp, weighed in shells

2 tablespoons butter

2 tablespoons chopped almonds

1 tablespoon flour

2 tablespoons curry powder

Salt and pepper

1 cup cream

3 tablespoons dry sherry

Rice pilaf

1 tablespoon minced parsley

Wash sea fruits; open them by putting in dry pan with lid over brisk fire. Remove meat and liquids, discard shells and keep meat tepid in their own liquid.

Cook shrimp in abundant well-salted water, then shell and devein them.

Heat butter in blazer pan of chafing dish and in it lightly toast the almonds; add flour and curry powder and toast 20 seconds.

Add 1 cup of liquid from sea fruits and bring to the boil, stirring constantly. Add salt and pepper to taste and cream. Bring to boil again. Add shrimp, sea fruits and sherry and warm through.

Serve on a bed of rice pilaf and sprinkle with parsley.

CRAB MAISON
[Serves 4]

1 tablespoon butter

1 tablespoon minced shallots or green onions

1 tablespoon chopped parsley or 1 teaspoon parsley flakes

Pinch tarragon

¼ cup dry vermouth or white wine

1 10-ounce package frozen

artichoke hearts, thawed

¾ pound lump crab or 2 6-ounce packages frozen crabmeat, thawed and drained

2 egg yolks

½ cup light cream

Thin slices French bread, buttered and toasted in broiler

⅛ teaspoon Tabasco sauce

Melt butter in blazer pan directly over flame and sauté shallots, parsley and tarragon for 1 minute. Add vermouth and boil until it is reduced to half, about 6 minutes.

Meanwhile, pour boiling water over artichoke hearts to partially cook. Add drained crab and artichoke hearts to blazer pan and simmer until crab is cooked, about 10 minutes.

Place blazer pan over boiling water in lower pan.

Beat egg yolks with cream and Tabasco and add to crab all at once. Cook, stirring constantly, until mixture is hot and slightly thickened but not boiling.

Serve on toasted French bread.

Ever think of toting a chafing dish to a picnic? Why not? After all you need no gas or electricity—just a little can of Sterno.

That's what Alice Stanley used to do in New England. And her specialty was

SHRIMP WIGGLE
[Serves 4]

1 6-ounce can shrimp	2 cups (1 pint) milk
2 tablespoons butter	1 8-ounce can little peas
2 tablespoons flour	Salt and pepper to taste
1 slice pimiento, cut fine	1 package soda crackers

Slice cleaned shrimp in half.

Melt butter; add flour and pimiento and stir well, cooking for 3 minutes. Add milk slowly, stirring constantly, cooking until thick, about 10 minutes. Add shrimp and peas and heat through. Season with salt and pepper.

Alice: "We poured the goo over the crackers, added a dill pickle or a lemon slice, a bottle of Moxie—and had a beach feast."

Later on, Alice went epicure:

SHRIMP SLITHER
[Serves 4]

½ pound fresh shrimp
4 tablespoons butter
4 tablespoons flour
1 pint cream
½ pound fresh green peas, slightly precooked

¼ cup sliced stuffed green olives
1 cup button mushrooms, lightly browned
Salt and pepper to taste
Paprika

4 pastry shells

Clean, devein and remove tails of shrimp; cut in half.
Melt butter in chafing dish, add flour and blend well. Add cream and bring to boil, by which time it has thickened. Add shrimp, peas, olives, and mushrooms. Season. Possibly add a sprinkle of grated Parmesan cheese. Top with paprika. ("To take away that pappy, naked look cream dishes always have," Alice says.) Pour into pastry shells.

"Of course," she adds, "this is pretty darned expensive, now. But you can always go back to the beach-picnic version."

SOUTH SEA SHRIMP
[Serves 4]

¼ cup (½ stick) butter or margarine
½ cup chopped sweet peppers
½ cup peeled, seeded and chopped cucumber
1 clove garlic, minced
2 cups sour cream

1 tablespoon chopped chutney
2 teaspoons lemon juice
2 teaspoons curry powder
½ teaspoon ginger
3 cups cooked, shelled and deveined shrimp

½ teaspoon salt

Have all ingredients at hand and laid out in order of their use.

Melt butter in blazer pan over medium flame. Add peppers, cucumber, and garlic and cook until tender but do not brown.

Place blazer pan over boiling water in lower pan. Stir in remaining ingredients in order given. Cook, stirring once in a while, until mixture is heated through. Serve over hot fluffy rice.

This is a favorite recipe of author John Milton Hagen of Mill Valley, Calif.

JAPANESE SHRIMP
[Serves 10 or 12 as appetizers]

2 pounds shrimp	Pinch salt
1 tablespoon melted butter	½ can condensed cream of
2 eggs	mushroom soup
1 teaspoon baking powder	Cooking oil

Clean and rinse peeled shrimp; split down back so they will open flat, butterfly fashion, leaving tails intact.

Mix butter into eggs. Mix baking powder and salt into undiluted soup, then combine all and beat until batter is smooth.

Heat cooking oil in blazer pan of chafing dish until it is quite hot.

Dip shrimp in batter and fry in oil until brown, from 4 to 5 minutes.

Variations: Vegetables, such as cubed eggplant, strips of green pepper, or cauliflowerets may be fried in the oil after dipping in the above batter.

Mimi Kilgore is the wife of a San Francisco surgeon and her dinners frequently have to wait for the late, late doctor. So she frequently plans meals that can be partly prepared ahead of time and then finished in chafing dishes.

Here is one, a buffet supper served with a tossed salad (lettuce, mandarin oranges, minced celery and watercress and classic French dressing), long stemmed strawberries dipped in confectioners' sugar, a dry white wine like an aromatic Semillon, and

MIMI'S SHRIMP CURRY
[Serves 10]

Spice bag

2 lemons, sliced
1 large onion, sliced
4 cloves garlic
1 tablespoon whole allspice
1 tablespoon salt

1 teaspoon peppercorns
1 teaspoon whole cloves
1 teaspoon crushed, dried red
    pepper
2 bay leaves

3 pounds shrimp, shelled
    and deveined, fresh or
    frozen
3 tablespoons butter
1½ cups fine-chopped onions
2 tablespoons best curry
    powder

3 cans frozen cream of
    shrimp soup, thawed
⅓ cup heavy cream
3 cups sour cream
3 tablespoons sherry
Hot rice

Condiments

Chopped cashew nuts
Chopped hard-cooked egg
Blond raisins

Flaked coconut
Chutney

Tie spices securely in cheesecloth and simmer in enough boiling water to cover shrimp for 15 minutes.

If shrimp is frozen, thaw. Add shrimp to pot and simmer 5 to 10 minutes, covered. Remove pan from heat and let shrimp stand in hot liquid 5 minutes. Drain.

Melt butter in large skillet, add onions and curry powder and cook until onions are tender. Remove skillet from heat and blend in soup and cream. Add shrimp and place all in top of double boiler over simmering water and cook, stirring, until hot. Fold in sour cream and sherry and continue cooking until hot, stirring constantly.

Pour into chafing dish and serve over hot rice, with condiments on the side.

Mimi usually simmers shrimp the day before and lets them remain overnight in the refrigerator with the spice bag, covered.

And here is another Kilgore version of curried shrimp.

SHRIMP CURRY A LA TIBURON
[Serves 8 to 10]

3½ to 4 pounds large shrimp, shelled and deveined, fresh or frozen
4 tablespoons butter
4 tablespoons flour
2 teaspoons curry powder
1 teaspoon salt

Dash cayenne
2 cups hot chicken stock or consommé
4 bananas
1 tablespoon sherry
Hot fluffy rice
Minced parsley

Cook shrimp exactly like preceding recipe, using same spice bag.

Melt butter in blazer pan. Remove from heat and stir in flour, curry, salt and cayenne. Gradually add chicken stock, stirring until smooth.

Return pan to heat and cook, stirring constantly until sauce is thickened.

Peel bananas; cut in half crosswise, then split halves. Add to sauce, cover and cook until bananas are tender. Add shrimp and sherry and heat through.

Serve on rice; sprinkle parsley over.

In Washington, Rosemary Cartwright makes the following dish in a Chinese wok, but says it can be done just as well in a chafing dish at table.

CHINESE SHRIMP BALLS
[Makes about 40]

3 pounds raw shrimp, cleaned, deveined and shelled
¼ pound pork fat
3 tablespoons chopped water chestnuts
3 tablespoons chopped bamboo shoots

4 unbeaten egg whites
½ teaspoon salt
¼ teaspoon white pepper
Dash soy sauce
½ cup sifted flour
Ice water
⅓ cup cornstarch
Cooking oil

Combine shrimp, fat, water chestnuts, and bamboo shoots and chop together until very fine. Stir in egg whites, salt, pepper, soy sauce, flour and only enough ice water to make material hold together. Mix with hands and knead until it can be formed into walnut-sized balls. Roll in cornstarch.

Heat oil to sizzling in blazer pan over direct flame. Add shrimp balls, half at a time, and deep fry until browned on all sides. Serve immediately.

SHRIMPERS AND RICE
[Serves 4 generously]

1 small onion, fine-chopped
2 ounces (½ stick) butter
1 10½-ounce can minced clams
2 pimientos, cut in small strips
¼ cup minced parsley
½ teaspoon salt
¼ teaspoon fresh-crushed pepper
1⅓ cups packaged precooked rice
1 10-ounce box frozen cleaned, shelled shrimp, cooked

Cook onion in butter which has been melted in top or blazer pan over direct heat until onion is almost tender, about 10 minutes.

Drain clams and to clam juice add enough water to make 1½ cups. Add this to onion, along with pimientos and parsley. Heat and bring to a boil.

Put over boiling water, add seasonings and stir in rice with fork. Cover and let stand 5 minutes. Add clams and shrimp and heat well.

SHRIMP PROVENCALE
[Serves 8 as appetizer]

4 tablespoons butter or margarine
1 clove garlic
1 pound small shrimp, shelled and deveined
1 green onion, minced
½ teaspoon salt
4 peppercorns
2 tablespoons chopped parsley

Melt butter in blazer pan over direct flame.

Pierce garlic clove with toothpick and add to butter with shrimp, onion, salt and peppercorns. Stir occasionally and as steam rises, cover and simmer gently over low flame until shrimp turn pink, 5 minutes for fresh shrimp and 10 for frozen.

Remove garlic clove and sprinkle with parsley. Serve with cocktail picks.

SCALLOPS PROVENCALE
[Serves 4 to 6]

2 pounds bay scallops
Flour (about ⅓ cup)
2 tablespoons seasoned
    stuffing mix, crushed

⅔ cup olive oil
2 garlic cloves, minced
Salt and pepper
¼ cup minced parsley
Lemon wedges

Rinse scallops and pat dry with paper towels. Roll in mixed flour and crushed stuffing.

In top pan of chafing dish, heat oil over medium flame; add scallops and cook 3 to 4 minutes, stirring and turning gently all the time. After a minute of stirring, add garlic. Season to taste with salt and pepper, add parsley and serve at once with lemon wedges.

Ira Dole has spent almost half his life as executive chef of that celebrated Western watering hole, the Brown Palace Hotel in Denver. One of his specialties is a fish of the region—Boned Rocky Mountain Trout. If you don't happen to have any in your local trout stream or kitchen freezer, make do with filet of gray sole, whitefish or perch.

ROCKY MOUNTAIN RAINBOW TROUT
[Serves 4]

4 rainbow trout, 12 ounces
    each, split and boned
1½ teaspoons salt
¼ teaspoon pepper
Flour
4 eggs

½ cup light cream
½ cup butter
32 whole baby carrots,
    cooked
32 small potato balls, cooked
Trout Sauce (see below)

Prepare fish in kitchen. Sprinkle with salt and pepper;
dip into flour and shake off any excess.

Beat eggs with cream. Dip fish into egg mixture and
place on wire rack to drain.

Bring fish to table on platter.

Heat butter, ¼ cup at a time, in blazer pan over
medium-high flame. Add half of fish, fleshy side down
and cook until golden, turn and cook other side until
golden brown and fish flakes easily with fork, about 5
minutes per side. Transfer to heated platter and repeat
with remaining butter and fish. Add carrots and potato
balls and heat through. Transfer them to the fish platter
and pour Trout Sauce over all.

TROUT SAUCE

4 ounces (1 stick) butter
4 ounces thinly sliced
    blanched almonds

⅔ cup lemon juice
¼ cup chopped parsley

Heat butter in saucepan; add almonds and cook until
lightly browned. Stir in lemon juice and parsley. Keep
warm until ready to serve.

TROUT WITH ALMONDS
[Serves 4]

4 trout, cleaned
2 tablespoons seasoned flour
3 ounces butter
3 ounces flaked almonds

1 tablespoon olive or cooking
    oil
2 tablespoons lemon juice
Parsley sprigs

Beforehand, toss the fish with the flour in paper bag. Bring to table along with remaining ingredients.

In blazer pan over medium heat, melt 1 ounce of the butter and fry the flaked almonds until they are lightly browned. Remove nuts from pan and reserve.

Add remaining butter to pan along with oil and heat. Fry trout gently until browned, about 5 minutes per side.

Serve on warmed plates with browned almonds, lemon juice and parsley.

SOLE WITH ALMONDS
[Serves 4]

1½ pounds filet of sole (about 6 pieces)	½ cup cooking oil
	Juice of ½ lemon
Salt and pepper	1 teaspoon parsley
½ cup milk	3 tablespoons toasted
3 tablespoons flour	almonds
2 tablespoons whole butter	

Beforehand, clean and bone sole, divide into pieces, salt and pepper to taste; dip into milk and roll in flour.

In blazer pan over medium heat, cook oil until hot and fry fish pieces until golden brown on both sides. Arrange on heated plate. Sprinkle with lemon juice, parsley and toasted almonds.

In drained blazer pan, make *beurre noisette* by melting and heating butter until nut-colored. Pour over fish.

Serve with boiled or French-fried potatoes.

FILETS OF SOLE WITH PARMESAN
[Serves 4]

4 filets of sole	4 tablespoons butter
½ teaspoon salt	½ cup grated Parmesan
¼ teaspoon ground black pepper	cheese
	¼ cup clam juice

Beforehand, wash filets and let dry; season with salt and pepper.

In 2 tablespoons of the butter, sauté the fish until browned on both sides, in blazer pan over medium direct heat. Sprinkle with cheese and distribute remaining 2 tablespoons butter over filets. Add clam juice and simmer over low heat 5 minutes. Serve hot.

TUNA RABBIT
[Serves 4]

1 tablespoon butter
1 tablespoon flour
1 cup milk
1/8 teaspoon salt
1/8 teaspoon white pepper

1 cup diced American or
   Cheddar cheese
1 teaspoon Worcestershire
   sauce
1 cup (1 can) flaked tuna

Melt butter in blazer pan over direct heat, stir in flour; gradually stir in milk, stirring till mixture boils and thickens, then cook 3 minutes longer, stirring occasionally. Add seasonings and blend. Add cheese and Worcestershire and cook until cheese melts and mixture is smooth, stirring constantly. Add tuna and heat thoroughly, about 5 minutes more.

Serve over white, wholewheat or rye toast.

One of the most delightfully alive persons I've ever met is Hester Marsden-Smedley, a Londoner who bustles around the world, writing articles and books, delivering talks and good deeds from Chelsea to the Congo, from Australia to Samoa and from Dorset to the West Indies. When I asked her for a chafing dish recipe, she sent me this one as dished up on the island of Nevis where her family, the Pinneys, had Morning Star Plantation.

SEAFOOD MORNING STAR
[Serves 6 to 8]

3 tablespoons butter
2 pounds scallops or scampi, in chunks
1 pound green peppers, sliced
½ pound fruit (pawpaw, melon, peaches) in chunks
¼ pound onions, minced

Suspicion of garlic
Salt to taste
Touch saffron or turmeric
Pinch mixed spices
Pinch fresh or dried tarragon (or thyme or marjoram)
1 tablespoon cream
Dash rum

Melt butter in hot blazer pan until it froths. Toss in seafood, shake in the butter 2 minutes if raw, 1 minute if cooked or canned. Remove seafood from butter and keep warm.

Add peppers and fruit, onions and garlic to pan. Sprinkle with salt, saffron, mixed spices, and tarragon and shake until saturated, about 3 minutes. Stir and when mixture is very hot return seafood to pan. Add cream and rum and mix well. Heat very hot, but do not overcook seafood.

Can be served on toast or with hot cooked rice, either mixed into chafing dish or placed on warmed plates.

Any firm, fresh fish can be used instead of seafood and most fruits go well.

STUFFED FISH FILETS IN SHRIMP SAUCE
[Serves 4]

1 cup packaged stuffing mix
1 teaspoon anchovy paste
1 small onion, minced
¼ cup green olives, chopped fine
1 pound (4) fish filets

1 tablespoon butter or margarine
1 clove garlic, minced
1 tablespoon parsley, minced
1 can frozen shrimp bisque soup

⅓ cup milk

Combine stuffing mix, anchovy paste, onion, and olives. Place ¼ of mixture on each filet. Fold over into rolls and secure with toothpicks. Refrigerate until ready to use.

Melt butter in top pan of chafing dish over direct, medium flame. Add garlic and parsley. Stir in soup and milk and heat through. Place fish rolls in sauce. Spoon sauce over. Cover and reduce flame to low. Cook fish 10 to 15 minutes until done. Do not overcook; fish should be white and flaky.

Meat in Your Chafing Dish

CHICKENS AND OTHER BIRDS

This is the way chicken is cooked and served at my daughter's home. As she lives in Paris, there is no apology for the lavish use of champagne.

CHICKEN WITH CHAMPAGNE
[Serves 4]

Salt
1 3-pound young chicken
Champagne Sauce (see below)

2 tablespoons butter
2 cups dry champagne

Salt inside of chicken, truss and place in oven-proof casserole or Dutch oven. Butter top of chicken and pour champagne over. Bake in preheated 350° oven, basting every 10 minutes and turning until chicken is golden brown all over and tender, about 90 minutes. Remove chicken from casserole, untruss and keep warm until serving time.

CHAMPAGNE SAUCE

Drippings from baked chicken
4 cups heavy cream
3 shallots (or green onions) minced

4 large mushrooms, minced
1 sprig parsley, chopped
2 bay leaves
$1/8$ teaspoon powdered thyme
2 tablespoons butter
$3/4$ cup dry champagne

To drippings in baking dish, add cream, shallots, mushrooms, parsley, bay leaves, and thyme. Place over low heat and simmer, stirring often, until sauce is reduced to ⅔, about 10 or 12 minutes. Strain through fine sieve.

Pour sauce into blazer pan of chafing dish and place over boiling water. Stir in butter and champagne and blend and heat well.

Sauce may be served over chicken or in sauce boat separately after bird has been carved.

Recipe believed to have originated at Châlons-sur-Marne in the Champagne country.

Here is the way Rhea Wachsman prepares her culinary brain-child when she is in a hurry.

CHAFING DISH CHICKEN PACIFIC
[Serves 4]

2 barbecued chickens, quartered	½ cup water
	¼ cup soy sauce
1½ cups muscatel wine	Chutney sauce
Hot rice	

Arrange chicken quarters in chafing dish blazer pan over hot or boiling water. Add wine and water and heat. Sprinkle with soy sauce and heat through.

Glaze with chutney sauce (Rhea uses Raffetto's). Cook, basting frequently until sauce is well blended, about 10 minutes.

Serve chicken and sauce over mounds of rice.

Named for the Paris culinary journalist, Maurice Bles-teau.

SCHNITZEL A LA BLESTEAU
[Serves 4]

4 large chicken breasts	½ stick butter
Flour	4 whole eggs
Egg yolk	4 lemon slices, trimmed
Salt and pepper	4 anchovy filets
Breadcrumbs	4 pimiento strips
Paprika	

Flatten chicken breasts; dip in flour, then in egg yolk seasoned with salt and pepper, then in breadcrumbs. Brown breasts in butter, reduce heat and cook until tender; remove to hot dish.

Fry eggs separately in same pan, placing one egg on each breast. Trim rind from lemon slices and place one on each egg, then decorate with anchovy filets and pimiento. Sprinkle paprika over and serve at once.

CHICKEN BONNIE
[Serves 4]

2 large chicken breasts, boned	1 1-pound can pineapple chunks, drained
3 tablespoons butter or margarine	1 cup water
1 teaspoon salt	2 chicken bouillon cubes
¼ teaspoon fresh-ground pepper	½ teaspoon dried leaf thyme
2 stalks celery, cut diagonally	½ teaspoon parsley flakes
2 green onions, sliced	1 tablespoon cornstarch
	1 pimiento or sweet red pepper, diced
1 small avocado, diced	

Remove skin from boned chicken breasts and cut into halves. Cut each half in 10 or 12 strips.

Assemble other ingredients on tray.

Melt butter in blazer pan directly over flame; add chicken, sprinkle with salt and pepper. Cook, stirring often, until chicken loses its color, about 6 or 7 minutes.

Add celery, onions, pineapple, water, bouillon cubes, thyme and parsley. Bring to boil and simmer 15 minutes, until chicken is almost tender.

Place over boiling water pan.

Blend together cornstarch and 1 tablespoon water, stir into blazer pan and cook until thickened. Add pimiento and avocado.

Serve over rice.

The Ciprianis have the loveliest, most relaxing hotel in Venice and that gem of hospitality and great kitchen—Harry's Bar.

POLLO ALLA CIPRIANI
[Serves 2]

2 chicken breasts, each sliced in 2
Salt, pepper, paprika

1 tablespoon butter
½ cup currant jelly
½ cup (4 ounces) Marsala

Anoint chicken with seasonings.

In blazer pan of chafing dish over direct flame, melt butter; brown chicken on both sides. Add jelly and cook until chicken is tender, about 15 minutes. At that point add wine and serve over buttered, hot *al dente* pasta.

Al dente, to the tooth, describes pasta which has been cooked only long enough to make it slightly resistant when you chew it.

CHICKEN A LA KING
[Serves 4]

3 ounces butter or chicken
    fat
½ cup sliced mushrooms
¼ cup bell pepper in
    diamond shapes
½ cup sherry
2 cups Cream Sauce (see
    below)
½ cup heavy cream
2 cups coarsely diced cooked
    chicken

2 tablespoons pimiento, in
    diamond shapes
⅛ teaspoon cayenne
Salt
2 egg yolks
Toasted slivered almonds
    (optional)
Flaky Pastry Shells (see
    below)
White seedless grapes
    (optional)

Cream

Heat butter or chicken fat in large blazer pan; add mushrooms and peppers; sauté about 4 minutes over low heat. Add sherry and cook until liquid is reduced by ⅓. Blend Cream Sauce and heavy cream, mix well and simmer 3 minutes more. Now add chicken, pimiento, cayenne and salt to taste; simmer about 4 or 5 minutes more, still over low heat. Thicken with egg yolks that have been mixed with a little cream. Serve on Flaky Pastry Shells, toast, noodle nests, cornbread or croutons. An elegant touch is to garnish each serving with toasted, slivered almonds and white seedless grapes.

CREAM SAUCE
[Makes 2 cups]

2 tablespoons butter
4 tablespoons flour

2 cups hot milk
Pinch salt

Pinch nutmeg

Heat butter; add 4 level tablespoons flour; stir well until all lumps are gone and mixture is smooth; add milk, salt and nutmeg; cook, stirring occasionally, an additional 18 minutes. Strain through fine sieve.

FLAKY PASTRY SHELLS
[Makes 4 large shells]

1½ cups flour
  Generous pinch salt

⅔ cup shortening
  Cold water

Sift flour and salt together; cut in half of the shortening with pastry blender or 2 knives; add enough water (around 3 tablespoons) to hold ingredients together, sprinkling the water evenly and mixing with fork to make ball. Wrap in waxed paper, place in refrigerator and chill for 20 minutes.

On a lightly-floured board roll ball out to oblong ¼ inch thick. Spread with half the remaining shortening, fold to make 3 layers; turn ¼ of the way around, roll out again to ¼-inch thickness, spread with half the remaining shortening, and fold into 3 layers; turn ¼ of the way around, roll out again to ¼-inch thickness, spread with remaining shortening and fold into three layers. Wrap in waxed paper and chill again.

Roll out on floured board to ¼-inch thickness; cut into rounds about 2 inches wider than diameter of good-sized pastry pans. Fit dough over inverted pans and trim edges. Prick through bottom and sides of dough with fork. Bake in 450° oven until done, 10 to 15 minutes.

As served at Luchow's . . .

CHICKEN A LA KING NO. 2
[Serves 4]

2 large chicken breasts,
  boiled until very
  tender
2 tablespoons butter
4 large mushroom caps,
  chopped
1 green pepper, chopped

½ cup dry sherry
2½ cups light cream
3 egg yolks, lightly beaten
1 tablespoon chopped
  pimiento
4 slices buttered toast,
  trimmed

Salt and white pepper

Skin and bone chicken breasts and cut into 1-inch pieces.

In chafing dish, melt butter and sauté mushrooms and green pepper until tender. Remove from heat and stir in ¼ cup of the sherry. Bring to boil over heat again. Slowly stir in 2 cups of the cream and simmer, stirring constantly until cream thickens slightly, 2 or 3 minutes. Add chicken cubes and simmer 2 minutes more.

Blend egg yolks and remaining ½ cup of the cream in bowl. Add some of chicken mixture, stir well, then add egg mixture to chicken mixture in chafing dish. Add pimiento, salt and pepper to taste.

Just before serving, stir in remaining ¼ cup sherry. Cut toast diagonally and place on hot serving plates. Pour chicken over.

CHICKEN HASH SUPREME
[Serves 4]

4 cups cream	Salt and fresh-ground
2 cooked chicken breasts,	pepper
diced fine	6 egg yolks
2 tablespoons dry sherry	

Bring cream to a gentle boil in a large blazer pan. Add chicken. Simmer for about 4 minutes on low fire. Salt and pepper to taste. Thicken with egg yolks that have been mixed with a little of cream. Just before serving, mix in the sherry. Serve on thin toast.

John Philips Cranwell, a culinary Marco Polo with headquarters in Washington, D.C., sends on this unusual Japanese recipe he found in Hakone. Doubtful if the majority of the ingredients can be found in the average U.S. kitchen, so a visit to your nearest Japanese grocery is advised before starting.

YOSENABE
[Serves 4]

2 boned chicken breasts, cut in ⅓rds

1 quart *dashi no moto* (clear broth made like tea with bag immersed in boiling water)

20 slices large white radish (or turnips)

20 slices large carrot (⅛ inch thick)

½ cup *Mirin,* a kind of sake used in cooking

¼ cup *sho you* sauce, a Japanese soy sauce

8 thin scallions in 1-inch lengths

12 cubes bean curd

½ pound *kon-nyaku,* clear potato noodles

36 raw oysters

20 pieces *nori,* seaweed which comes in very thin sheets and is cut into 2-inch squares

16 small pieces raw codfish

16 small squares raw squid

1 can heart of palm, sliced thin

12 medium mushrooms, stemmed and halved

The dramatis personae are awesome but the dish is simple.

Cook chicken breasts in *dashi no moto* until almost tender, adding radish or turnips and carrot for last 5 minutes.

Then, put all ingredients in a ceramic casserole which can be placed directly on an hibachi or small electric stove on the dining table (or a large chafing dish with a cover to fit).

Cover the casserole and place over heat. Stir occasionally until broth simmers well. A few cups of hot sake will pass the time until the steam starts. The Yosenabe is now ready. Remove lid from casserole and do not re-cover.

Ladle some of broth into small individual lacquer bowls. Each guest then helps himself, with chopsticks of course, to whatever tidbits he likes—the oysters are superb—places them in his bowl, and eats the solid food with occasional sips of the broth directly from the bowl.

After the food is consumed you may, as the Japanese do, add a bowl of steamed rice to the casserole and go on eating until the utensil is empty.

You can drink beer with the dish, but hot sake is much better.

Follow with a pot of very hot green tea.
Okaka ga suita, or *bon appétit!*

ROCK CORNISH HENS WITH A HOTFOOT
[Serves 4]

4 Rock Cornish hens, roasted
   according to package
   directions
2 tablespoons butter or
   margarine
½ cup red currant jelly
4 teaspoons lemon juice
3 tablespoons water

¾ teaspoon salt
⅛ teaspoon ground cloves
   Sprinkle fresh-ground
   pepper
½ cup Port wine
2 tablespoons pan gravy
   from hens
2 tablespoons brandy

Keep roasted hens warm on warm platter.

Put butter, jelly, lemon juice, water, salt, cloves and pepper into blazer pan and simmer 5 minutes. Stir in wine and pan gravy and simmer 3 minutes longer. Add brandy, ignite and when blaze dies, pour over hens, and serve immediately. Green beans with almonds go well with this. So does wild rice.

Do you have a Duck Press? In the wicked old days anyone with a chafing dish would be sure to have a duck press, too. It is a cylinder of handsome metal, with a little spout at the bottom and a screw and plunger top. You inserted the cooked carcass of the duck in the top—after carving off the breasts in thin slices—and turned the bar which sent the screw and plunger downward, squeezing all the juices out of the carcass through the little spout.

If you have no duck press, but your husband has something in his workshop which will do the job, then this is your dish:

PRESSED DUCK
[Serves 4]

2 mallard ducks, prepared for
   roasting
Salt and cayenne pepper

3 tablespoons grated orange
   peel
2 tablespoons sherry

Roast ducks 20 minutes in hot oven. Bring to table immediately. Carve off legs and reserve meat. Carve thin slices from breasts and place in blazer pan of chafing dish.

Squeeze out juices in carcass of each duck in press or otherwise. Salt and cayenne to taste is then added to juice. Add orange peel and sherry to juice, stir and add to slices of duck in pan and heat, but do not boil.

Duck slices may be flamed by adding 2 ounces warmed brandy just before serving.

Variation: While pressing carcasses, add 1 wine glass dry red wine to each.

DUCK MARYLAND SHORE STYLE
[Serves 4]

2 wild ducks, prepared for cooking	1 tablespoon celery leaves
Salt and pepper	2 tablespoons tart currant jelly
2 tablespoons butter	3 ounces dry red wine

Preheat oven to 500°. Sprinkle ducks with salt and pepper and roast in shallow pan 20 minutes.

Carve off each breast in 1 whole serving piece; disjoint drumsticks; reserve livers. Use rest of carcass for soup, etc.

In chafing dish blazer or suzette pan, heat butter to foaming over highest heat; transfer scrapings, blood and essence from roasting pan to chafing dish pan, add 4 duck breasts and drumsticks, sear meat rapidly, turning often, until medium rare, 6 to 8 minutes, and remove to warm plates.

Add to chafing dish reserved duck livers, crushed; celery leaves, jelly and wine. Cook up fast and divide over duck breasts.

BEEF RECIPES, STARTING WITH CHAFING DISH STEAKS

From René Lasserre's 3-star restaurant in Paris:

STEAK DUMAS
[Serves 4]

4 5- to 6-ounce sirloin tenderloin steaks, cut thin
Salt and fresh-ground pepper
Butter
12 slices beef marrow, ¾ inches thick, poached in boiling water for 3 minutes
½ pint dry wine
2 tablespoons chopped scallions
¼ pound butter
1 tablespoon minced parsley

Season steaks with salt and fresh-ground pepper, cook to desired finish in butter in blazer pan. Remove to heated serving platter and place 3 slices of beef marrow on each. Keep warm.

Add wine and scallions to blazer pan, heat to boil and reduce sauce by ¾ths. Remove from heat, add butter, blend well and taste for seasoning.

Sprinkle ground pepper and parsley on top of marrow, then coat steaks with sauce. Serve very hot.

Here is one of the easiest and best ways to serve steaks, be they sirloin, New York cut, or rib eye. It is the way they are served at that fashionable and excellent restaurant, Quo Vadis, in New York.

STEAK DIANE
[Serves 1]

1 12-ounce sirloin steak
Salt and fresh-ground pepper
2 tablespoons butter
1 teaspoon chopped shallots
1 teaspoon minced chives
½ teaspoon Worcestershire sauce
1 tablespoon A.1. sauce
Chopped parsley
2 tablespoons cognac

Trim all fat from steak and pound it evenly, between 2 sheets of waxed paper to prevent breaking, until it is very, very thin. Sprinkle steak well with salt and pepper on one side.

In chafing dish blazer pan melt 1 tablespoon of the butter and sauté shallots in it; add the steak, sear it quickly on both sides, adding more salt and pepper as desired. With fork and spoon, roll steak over and remove to warmed dish.

Melt the second tablespoon of butter in pan juices, add chives, cook for 1 minute, then add Worcestershire and A.1. Blend well and cook until sauce thickens, but do not boil. Return steak to pan, sprinkle 1 side with parsley, turn and do the same on other side.

Warm cognac in small pot or pan, add to chafing dish and set ablaze.

When flames die out, serve steak and pour sauce over it.

FLAMING FILETS MIGNON
[Serves 4]

4 filets of beef tenderloin, 1½ inches thick	4 slices bread
	Butter
1 clove garlic split in half	4 teaspoons brandy, warmed
Salt and fresh-ground pepper	Watercress
	Broiled tomatoes

Souffléed potatoes

Rub filets all over with cut side of garlic; season well with salt and pepper.

Cut bread to size of filets, sauté in butter in blazer pan until crisp and brown on both sides. Remove and keep warm.

In same pan, cook filets in hot butter over high heat until very brown on outside but rare inside. Lift filets and put fried bread under them. Add more melted butter to pan. Pour in warmed brandy, light and shake pan until flame dies.

Transfer bread and filets to large, hot platter; pour pan juices over and garnish with watercress, broiled tomatoes and souffléed potatoes.

TOURNEDOS HUNTER STYLE
[Serves 4]

1 cup sliced mushrooms	bouillon
1 tablespoon minced	1 cup tomato sauce
shallots	1 tablespoon chopped
5 tablespoons butter	parsley
Salt and white pepper	1½ pound beef tenderloin in
1 cup dry white wine	tournedos (round
1 cup beef stock or	medallions)

First prepare Hunter Sauce by frying mushrooms and shallots in half the butter in blazer pan, seasoning with salt and white pepper. Add wine, stock and tomato sauce and simmer 5 minutes, then stir in parsley. Remove to warm sauce boat.

Season tournedos with salt and pepper. Sauté in remaining butter 2 to 4 minutes on each side, according to preference.

Remove to hot platter and pour Hunter Sauce over.

PEPPER STEAKS
[Serves 4]

4 8-ounce boneless rib	margarine
steaks	Tabasco sauce
Fresh-ground pepper	Worcestershire sauce
Salt	Lemon juice
4 tablespoons butter or	1½ ounces cognac or brandy
Minced parsley and chives	

Sprinkle each steak on both sides very liberally with pepper, pressing or pounding the pepper bits into the meat. Refrigerate ½ hour or more.

Sprinkle a light layer of salt (preferably coarse or kosher salt) over bottom of large blazer pan over direct flame and heat until salt begins to brown. Add steaks and cook at high heat until browned on one side—rare, 1 minute; better done, longer. Turn and cook other side. Place 1 tablespoon butter on each steak, add Tabasco, Worcestershire and lemon juice to taste.

Warm cognac separately, add to steaks and ignite, shaking pan until flames die. Serve immediately on hot plates, dividing pan juice and sprinkling with parsley and chives.

A.1. STEAKS
[Serves 4]

1 clove garlic, sliced thin
1/4 cup olive oil
4 very thin boneless sirloin
  steaks (5 or 6 ounces
  each)
1/4 cup butter
1 teaspoon dry mustard

1/2 teaspoon salt
1/4 cup chopped
  parsley
1 teaspoon lemon juice
2 tablespoons A.1. sauce
1/4 teaspoon fresh-ground
  pepper

Marinate garlic in oil for 5 minutes, then brush steaks on both sides with oil.

In large blazer pan, stir together butter, mustard, salt. Heat and add parsley, blending well.

When butter bubbles place steaks in pan and turn over to coat both sides thoroughly. Cook slowly for 5 minutes; turn steaks and cook other side 3 minutes.

Remove steaks to hot plates.

Stir into the sauce in pan, the lemon juice, A.1. sauce and pepper; blend well and heat. Divide sauce over steaks and serve at once.

One of my favorite restaurants any place, for food and relaxation, is George's in Rome, which is owned and operated by Vernon Jarrat. Here are three of the recipes I wheedled out of him.

FILET ETNA
[Serves 1]

Clarified butter
Filet of beef

Salt and pepper
1 slice mozzarella cheese
4 cooked asparagus tips

Put chafing dish on the lamp; add butter.
Season filet with salt and pepper to taste.

When butter is sizzling, put in steak. When the first side has cooked, turn over. When the second side is ¾ths cooked, cover steak with the cheese and asparagus. Cover pan with cover or plate while steak finishes cooking.

When done, take chafing dish off lamp, but leave steak in pan for 5 minutes without removing cover before serving.

If you wish to cook more than one steak at one time, use large pan and increase quantities of butter, cheese and asparagus.

And another steak, this time with brandy.

FILET AU COGNAC
[Serves 1]

1 filet steak, fairly thick, trimmed	Clarified butter
1 clove garlic	1 tablespoon butter
Salt and fresh-ground pepper	1 sage leaf
	2 ounces warm brandy

Score steak with a knife, rub both sides with garlic and season well with salt and pepper.

Put about 2 tablespoons clarified butter in chafing dish over good flame and when butter starts to sizzle, put steak in.

Cooking is a matter of personal taste. The two important things are that the outside is cooked to be crisp, and once the filet is in the pan it isn't touched except to turn it over. Length of cooking time depends, naturally, on whether the steak is to be rare, medium rare, or medium inside.

When cooking is almost finished, put tablespoon of butter and sage leaf on top of steak. When this extra butter has melted, but before it has begun to fry, add warm brandy and ignite. Let the flames die out naturally, without covering pan.

Remove pan from fire, cover with lid or plate and leave steak inside for at least 5 minutes. This extra period is most important to produce a rich sauce-juice.

Serve as soon as steak is taken from the pan.

CALF'S KIDNEYS ROBERT
[Serves 4]

3 calf's kidneys, trimmed   Juice of 1 lemon
4 tablespoons (½ stick) butter   Salt and fresh-ground
2 tablespoons brandy   pepper
        1 tablespoon minced parsley

Cook kidneys, whole, in butter in chafing dish over fairly high heat no more than 3 minutes.

Remove kidneys from pan and put in brandy, being careful not to let it ignite. Cook the liquid until it is reduced by ⅓.

Cut kidneys into thick slices while they are still very hot. Return them to pan with butter and brandy and finish their cooking to the desired point, adding the lemon juice and salt and pepper to taste. Garnish with parsley.

The Jockey Club in Washington, D.C., strives to be the capital's version of New York's "21". One night late, when the Boeuf Bourguignon was all gone, one of the captains suggested to Rosemary Cartwright his own specialty. Being a keen recipe detective, Rosemary observed with Hawkshaw concentration and, when the dish proved delicious, came away with this report.

MINUTE STEAK, JOCKEY CLUB
[Serves 2]

1 shallot or large spring   2 small filets mignon or cube
    onion, chopped fine   steaks
2 tablespoons minced parsley   2 tablespoons cracked black
3 tablespoons butter   pepper
1 tablespoon Worcestershire   2 slices bread, crust removed
    sauce

Mix shallot and parsley.

Melt butter over low heat in blazer pan. Add shallot, parsley and Worcestershire sauce. When shallot is soft, put in steaks and cook over low heat about 1 minute. Turn and salt cooked side. Let cook another minute, or until steak is done to your taste. If medium-rare, 4 minutes in all; well-done, about 6.

Remove from pan, place on hot plates, sprinkle with pepper and serve on bread slice.

Earl Wilson once relayed his Beautiful Wife's recipe for her chicken-fried steak, which can be done easily in a chafing dish.

"First, pour two cups bourbon into the chef— Oops, that's the recipe for Texas Chili . . . Start over . . ."

STEAK COUNTRY STYLE
[Serves 4]

2 pounds round steak, cut in pieces ½-inch thick	Salt and pepper
4 tablespoons flour	2 tablespoons butter
	2 tablespoons shortening

Pound flour into steak ferociously with wooden mallet, saucer edge or baseball bat until flour is imbedded on both sides. Sprinkle with salt and pepper.

In large blazer pan of chafing dish, melt butter and shortening until sizzling. Add steaks and brown and turn, crusting on both sides until surface is like fried chicken.

Serve with mashed potatoes, using part of potato water to blend with juices in pan to make gravy.

When President Eisenhower was in Denver recovering from illness, Chef Ira Dole of the Brown Palace Hotel created this dish for a dinner in his honor. Ike was so delighted that he ordered Beef President the next day for breakfast—and also for lunch. Later when the President had Mr. Dole and other Brown Palace executives at his mountain camp, Eisenhower himself cooked the dish for them.

BEEF PRESIDENT
[Serves 2]

¾ pound thin slices (6) beef   2 tablespoons butter
    filet   6 carrots, sliced and cooked
         6 whole new potatoes, cooked

If filet is to be served rare, prepare entire dish in
chafing dish at table. If not, sauté meat lightly in butter
before bringing it to table.

Melt butter in blazer pan over canned heat. Add meat,
cooking on both sides to desired doneness. Add cooked
vegetables and heat. Transfer to heated plates and cover
with President Sauce (see below).

PRESIDENT SAUCE

2 tablespoons butter   2 tablespoons sherry
1 cup fresh mushrooms, sliced   1 cup brown gravy

Heat butter in saucepan; add mushrooms and cook
until just tender; stir in sherry and gravy; simmer until
thoroughly blended. Keep warm and spoon over cooked
filet and vegetables.

At the renowned Seehof Hotel in picturesque Davos,
Switzerland, the old wine cellar has been transformed
into La Bohème, a Swiss-Bohemian restaurant with a
highly sophisticated atmosphere.

There Chef de Service Aimone Mucci performs won-
ders with chafing dishes in which he concocts such specialties as

FILET OF BEEF A LA BOHEME
[Serves 4]

2 pounds filet of beef
Salt
2 tablespoons cognac, warmed
2 tablespoons butter
½ cup fine-chopped green pepper
½ cup fine-chopped onion
½ cup fine-chopped kernel corn

½ cup fine-chopped pimiento
½ cup dry red wine
¼ cup canned condensed beef bouillon
½ teaspoon paprika
⅛ teaspoon Tabasco sauce
⅛ teaspoon garlic powder (optional)
½ cup heavy cream, whipped
Hot fluffy rice

Cut beef into cubes ½ inch by ½ inch by ¾ inches.
Sprinkle salt over large blazer pan. Heat salt over high flame. Add beef and brown quickly on all sides. Add cognac and set ablaze.

After flames die down, remove beef to heated platter. In same pan heat butter, cook green pepper, onion, corn and pimiento over medium heat until crisp-tender. Add wine and bouillon and cook over high heat until liquid is almost evaporated. Add paprika, Tabasco, and garlic powder. Turn heat to very low, add whipped cream and heat very slowly. Combine beef with cream mixture, heat through and serve with the cooked rice.

This simple but delicious chafing dish version of Boeuf Stroganoff was created by a legendary Russian from Georgia named Samson Madagashvili and was given to me by Bernard Simon, a mutual friend, who lost track of the creator 25 years ago. Anyone seen him since?

BOEUF STROGANOFF A LA MADAGASHVILI
[Serves 8]

4 pounds tenderloin steak, trimmed of all fat
Salt and pepper
Butter

2 cups coarse-chopped onion
3 small cans button mushroom caps with liquid
1 cup sour cream

Cut steak into ½-inch cubes and season "emphatically" with salt and pepper.

In large, preferably old-fashioned black iron pan with high sides (like a dutch oven), melt enough butter to cover bottom to depth of ¼ inch. Cook onion in butter until translucent. Add meat cubes and brown over moderate heat on all sides for about 10 minutes, adding a little butter.

Transfer from pan to blazer pan of chafing dish over low heat and add mushrooms and about half the liquid from cans. Cook 8 minutes longer, then stir in the sour cream, stirring constantly for 2 minutes, until sour cream and other liquid becomes a well-mixed sauce.

Serve immediately, along with mashed potatoes.

BEEF WITH MUSHROOMS AND TOMATOES
[Serves 4 to 6]

¼ cup oil
1 teaspoon salt
⅛ teaspoon pepper
1½ pounds tender beef, sliced thin
1 chicken bouillon cube
¾ cup water
2 fresh tomatoes, cut in eighths
½ pound mushrooms, sliced
1 tablespoon cornstarch
1 tablespoon soy sauce
¼ cup water

Heat oil with salt and pepper in the top pan of chafing dish over direct, high flame. Add beef slices and sauté 1 minute, stirring constantly. Reduce flame to medium, add chicken bouillon cube which has been dissolved in ¾ cup water, tomatoes and mushrooms. Cover and cook 4 to 5 minutes, reducing flame to low.

Add cornstarch mixed with water and soy sauce, stirring constantly until mixture is smooth and thick.

Serve with rice.

Lois Mawby and Jane Bloom are two young friends I met at the Museum of Modern Art where our interest in old movies brought us together. When I asked them for their favorite recipe they came up with the one below, but had no name for it. In view of the ingredients and our mutual interest, I've dubbed it—

BEEF KEYE LUKE
[Serves 4]

Marinade:

½ cup dry sherry   ½ cup soy sauce
                    1 clove garlic

2 pounds round or sirloin   1 pound mushrooms
    steak, 1½ inches thick   1 small can water chestnuts,
1 medium eggplant   drained
                    2 tablespoons cooking oil

Combine marinade ingredients.

Trim fat from steak and slice into thin strips; place in shallow pan and pour marinade over; let soak at least 1 hour. Drain steak slices and reserve marinade.

Slice eggplant in two lengthwise, and remove seeds; peel and slice crosswise into thin strips. Slice mushrooms and water chestnuts.

About 20 minutes before serving time, heat cooking oil in chafing dish (or Chinese *wok*) on stove. Braise meat and eggplant, adding them alternately a little at a time and pushing cooked pieces to the sides. When all of meat and eggplant are braised, add mushrooms, chestnuts and marinade. Toss lightly and steam for 5 to 10 minutes. Remove from heat and place over water pan on burner at table.

Serve with rice and tossed salad.

Slicing can be done the morning or day before. If eggplant is prepared ahead, place in bowl and cover with slightly salted water and store in refrigerator.

This is an American version of the best-known Japanese dish in the Western world.

SUKIYAKI
[Serves 4]

1 cup chopped green onions or scallions
3 tablespoons butter
1 pound beefsteak, cut in thin, narrow strips
Salt and pepper to taste
½ pound thin-sliced mushrooms
½ cup sliced celery
1 pound (or 1 can, drained)
bean sprouts
¼ cup thin-sliced water chestnuts
2 tablespoons soy sauce
2 cups raw spinach, chopped
1 bouillon cube dissolved in 1½ cups boiling water
1½ cups precooked rice

Sauté ½ cup of the green onions in the butter in blazer pan until transparent.

Salt and pepper beef to taste and add to onion. Cook till meat is brown on all sides. Add mushrooms, celery, bean sprouts, water chestnuts and soy sauce and cook about 8 minutes. Add spinach and cook 2 minutes longer.

In saucepan make broth of bouillon and water. Stir in rice. Mix well.

Pour rice into blazer pan with beef mixture, sprinkle other ½ cup of green onions over; cover and simmer over low heat no more than 5 minutes.

Serve with more soy sauce on side.

VEAL IN THE CHAFER

FLAMING VEAL FILETS
[Serves 4]

4 tablespoons butter
1½ pounds veal, in 12 filets, salted and peppered
4 tablespoons brandy
1 bouillon cube dissolved
in 4 tablespoons hot water
3 tablespoons heavy cream, whipped
Pinch curry powder

Melt butter in blazer pan, add veal and sauté over high heat until light brown on both sides. Pour brandy over and flame, shaking pan to flavor meat.

When flames die, remove veal pieces to preheated platter and keep warm.

Add dissolved bouillon to sauce in pan, bring to boil, lower heat. Stir in cream and keep stirring until sauce is smooth. Before serving, whip in curry, then pour over filets.

Serve with egg noodles or rice.

BRANDIED VEAL
[Serves 4]

1 tablespoon butter	1 teaspoon minced parsley
1½ pounds very thin veal cutlets (8 to 10)	2 tablespoons brandy, warmed
Salt and white pepper	½ cup heavy cream

Melt butter in blazer pan over direct heat. Add veal and brown on both sides. Season with salt, white pepper and sprinkle with parsley. Add brandy and flame, allowing cutlets to scorch until flames die. Add cream and cook gently until meat is tender and sauce thickens.

The whole process takes less than 8 minutes.

LUCHOW'S VEAL SCHNITZEL
[Serves 4]

4 8-ounce veal cutlets	1 teaspoon salt
2 ounces butter	¼ teaspoon fresh-ground pepper
6 eggs	
1 tablespoon chopped chives	10 sliced mushrooms
8 stalks cooked asparagus	

Dry cutlets. In blazer pan, brown cutlets in butter on both sides, reduce heat and cook until tender; remove to hot plate and keep warm.

Beat eggs until frothy, add chives, salt, pepper and mushroom slices; pour into hot pan (from cutlets) and cook like scrambled eggs. Pour over cutlets. Garnish with asparagus and serve at once.

From Vanessi's Restaurant in San Francisco (and I don't know if it is still there) comes this '30's chafing dish.

VANESSI'S VEAL SCALOPPINI
[Serves 4]

2 pounds veal	1 clove garlic
Flour	1 pound fresh mushrooms
4 tablespoons butter	Salt and fresh-ground
1½ tablespoons olive oil	pepper
3 small shallots	Pinch rosemary
1 clove garlic	3 ounces Marsala

Pinch of chopped parsley

Cut veal in 2-inch squares and pound until ¼-inch thin. Dredge with flour.

Melt butter and heat olive oil in blazer pan until almost sputtering. Brown meat on both sides.

Chop shallots and garlic. Slice mushrooms. Add to veal along with salt and pepper to taste and rosemary. Let all brown gently, then add wine and parsley. Simmer 5 minutes.

Green peas and cottage-fried potatoes go well with this.

VEAL A LA CREME
[Serves 6]

2 pounds thin veal cutlets	½ teaspoon fresh-ground
3 tablespoons flour	pepper
2 tablespoons butter or	1 cup heavy cream
margarine	½ teaspoon dried leaf
1 teaspoon salt	thyme

½ teaspoon dried leaf tarragon

Cut veal into serving portions, cover each slice with waxed paper and pound with flat side of cleaver, wooden mallet or bottom of iron skillet until ⅛-inch thick. Dredge cutlets with flour.

Heat butter in large skillet, add cutlets, sprinkle with salt and pepper and brown lightly on both sides.

Remove cutlets to blazer pan of chafing dish over bottom section filled with hot water.

Stir cream, thyme and tarragon into skillet, heat slowly over low heat, stirring to blend in brown crust. When well blended, pour sauce over cutlets in blazer pan and heat through.

VEAL BIRDS
[Serves 4 to 6]

1½ pounds veal rump
¼ pound thin-sliced
   prosciutto or Smithfield
   ham

2 tablespoons chopped
   parsley
3 tablespoons grated
   Parmesan cheese

Olive oil

Have veal cut thin and flattened into 4-inch squares. Top each piece with a slice of prosciutto, sprinkle with parsley and cheese. Roll carefully, secure with toothpicks.

Heat oil in blazer pan; brown rolls quickly on both sides until golden brown and tender, about 5 minutes. Serve with Risotto alla Milanese.

CURRY OF MINCED VEAL
[Serves 4]

¼ cup butter
1 pound veal, julienned
2 tablespoons minced onion

Salt and pepper
1 cup Curry Sauce (see below)
½ cup heavy cream

Heat butter quite hot in blazer pan; add veal and onion and season with salt and pepper to taste; sauté until golden brown.

Add Curry Sauce and heavy cream, mix well and bring to slow, gentle boil. Usually served with rice.

CURRY SAUCE
[Makes about 7 cups]

2 carrots
1 large onion
1 apple, cored
3 outside stalks celery
1 clove garlic
2 sticks (½ pound) butter
1 cup flour
6 tablespoons curry powder
2 large, ripe tomatoes, chopped

2 tablespoons shredded coconut
2 pounds cracked veal, lamb, beef or chicken bones
2 quarts chicken stock or consommé
1 teaspoon whole black peppercorns
2 tablespoons chopped chutney
1 bay leaf

Chop carrots, onion, apple, celery and garlic. In saucepan, simmer in butter 5 minutes. Add flour, stir well and simmer a further 4 minutes. Add curry powder, tomatoes and coconut and mix. Add bones, stock, bay leaf, peppercorns and chutney. Cook 45 minutes to hour at low simmer. Taste and add salt if needed. Strain.

LAMB IN THE PAN

LAMB LEONARDO
[Serves 6]

2 pounds lamb steaks or shoulder
1 cup button mushrooms or 1 6-ounce can whole mushrooms, drained
¾ cup dry sherry

4 tablespoons minced parsley
1 cut clove garlic
6 tablespoons (¾ stick) butter or margarine
6 fresh sage leaves
6 slices Gruyère cheese

Cut lamb into 6 serving portions and pound under waxed paper until ¼-inch thick. Nick edges to prevent curling.

Mix mushrooms, sherry, parsley and garlic (pierced by toothpicks). Place meat in shallow pan and marinate with mixture for ½ hour or more, turning meat several times. Drain meat, saving marinade.

In blazer pan over direct heat, melt butter and quickly brown 3 slices lamb about 3 minutes on each side. Remove to warm platter and brown remaining 3 slices. Take first 3 slices from platter and add to pan. Add marinade, removing garlic, and bring to boil. Place sage leaf over each piece of meat, cover with slice of cheese that fits. Cover pan and cook over reduced heat until cheese melts, 2 or 3 minutes. Put meat back in warm serving dish and spoon hot marinade sauce over.

APPLE-CURRY SAUCE AND LAMB CHOPS
[Serves 4]

2 cups chopped apples	1 10½-ounce can or 1¼ cups
1 red onion, sliced	chicken broth
2 tablespoons shortening	⅓ cup Burgundy
3 tablespoons flour	1 tablespoon lemon juice
2 tablespoons curry powder	1 cup flaked coconut
½ teaspoon salt	4 double-cut lamb chops
¼ teaspoon fresh-ground	4 cups cooked, hot rice
pepper	¼ cup sautéed chopped
	parsley

Sauté apples and onions in shortening in blazer pan over direct medium-hot heat, until golden.

Blend flour, curry powder, salt and pepper; add broth, wine and lemon juice.

Stir into apple mixture, stirring until smooth. Cover and simmer at low heat for 15 to 20 minutes. Afterwards add coconut.

During that time, broil lamb chops 3 inches from source of heat for 10 to 12 minutes, turning once. Serve chops over rice-parsley mixture with sauce on the side.

Next is a chafing dish for lamb lovers from Vivien Dolan.

CUBED LAMB WITH RICE
[Serves 6]

4 tablespoons yellow corn-meal	2 pounds cooked lamb in cubes
2 teaspoons paprika	1 cup chopped onions
1 teaspoon seasoned salt	1 large can sliced mushrooms, drained
1 teaspoon seasoned pepper	
4 tablespoons cooking oil	2 cups water
Cooked rice	

Blend together cornmeal, paprika, salt and pepper.

Roll lamb in 2 tablespoons oil, then in cornmeal mixture and let stand 1 hour.

Place remaining 2 tablespoons oil in skillet, heat, add onions and cook until tender; add mushrooms and mix well. Add lamb and 2 cups water and simmer 20 minutes. Transfer to preheated chafing dish over hot water.

If you have two chafing dishes, keep cooked rice heated in second one.

Note: Raw lamb may be cooked in the same manner, only skip rolling cubes in oil before dredging in cornmeal mixture. And, of course, cook longer—until meat is tender.

LAMBURGERS
[Serves 4]

1 pound ground raw lamb	1½ teaspoons minced parsley
1 small onion, minced	1 cup soft breadcrumbs
1½ teaspoons salt	Dash Tabasco sauce
½ teaspoon fresh-ground pepper	Cooking oil

Mix lamb, onion, salt, pepper, parsley, crumbs and Tabasco. Add 2 tablespoons oil and shape into 4 patties.

Heat another 2 tablespoons of oil in blazer pan over direct heat and brown patties quickly on both sides in hot oil. Cut heat down, cover and cook slowly for 10 minutes, turning once.

Serve with catsup, chili sauce, Worcestershire, A.1. sauce or Mint Sauce.

A tasty way of fixing leftover lamb.

NEXT-DAY LAMB
[Serves 4]

2 tablespoons butter or
    margarine
1 cup sliced mushrooms
1 tablespoon minced onion

1 cup lamb gravy
8 slices roast lamb
1 tablespoon sherry
1 tablespoon Parmesan cheese

Melt butter in blazer pan over medium direct heat. Sauté mushrooms until lightly browned. Add onion, gravy, lamb, stir gently and heat well. Add wine and cheese; blend and heat again. Serve hot on hot plates.

LAMB HASH
[Serves 4]

2 tablespoons butter
1 small onion, minced
2 cups diced cooked lamb
¾ cup diced cooked potatoes
1 small pimiento, chopped
¾ cup lamb stock or broth

¾ cup evaporated milk,
    undiluted
2 small egg yolks, slightly
    beaten
Salt and fresh-ground
    pepper to taste

Melt butter in blazer pan over direct heat. Cook onion, stirring, 3 minutes. Add lamb, potato, pimiento and stock; bring to a boil.

Mix milk and egg yolks and season. Stir into hash and summer 4 or 5 minutes. Serve on hot plates.

PORK AND HAM ON THE TABLE

Here is a small selection of pork chafing dish recipes, small because pork takes thorough and long cooking, which is not for the chafing dish chef. As you see, most of these recipes call for precooked pork.

PORK TENDERLOIN VERONIQUE
[Serves 4]

4 serving portions pork
   tenderloin, 1/4-inch thick
Seasoned flour
6 tablespoons butter or
   margarine
1 cup seedless grapes

4 tablespoons Madeira or
   Marsala wine
1 tablespoon Worcestershire
   sauce
Salt and fresh-ground
   pepper to taste

1/2 cup cream

Shake tenderloin pieces lightly in paper bag with seasoned flour.

In blazer or crêpe pan over direct flame heat butter to point where it just begins to brown. Add meat and brown thoroughly on both sides until well done. Remove tenderloins to hot plates.

Quickly make Veronique Sauce. Put grapes in pan; add wine; heat and flame. When flames die down, add cream and Worcestershire, blend well, and season to taste. Heat through and pour sauce over meat. Serve immediately.

PORK, HONOLULU STYLE
[Serves 4]

1 1/2 pounds lean pork
   shoulder, in 1/2-inch
   strips
1 beaten egg
1 tablespoon milk
3 tablespoons flour
1/2 teaspoon salt
3 tablespoons butter or
   margarine
1 peeled clove garlic,
   pierced by toothpick
1 bouillon cube dissolved

in 1 cup hot water
1 cup pineapple tidbits
1/2 cup pineapple juice
1 sliced carrot
1 green pepper, sliced
2 tablespoons wine vinegar
2 tablespoons soy sauce
1 tablespoon sugar
2 tablespoons cornstarch,
   stirred into paste in
   cold water
Hot fluffy rice

Cut pork strips into 2-inch lengths.

Mix egg, milk, flour and salt together until smooth. Coat pork strips with mixture and fry in butter or margarine in blazer pan over direct heat until browned and cooked thoroughly. During this time, add garlic clove for 2 minutes, then remove.

Remove meat to warm platter and place in blazer pan the bouillon, pineapple juice, carrot, pepper, vinegar, soy sauce and sugar; simmer 5 minutes. Return meat to pan, thicken with the cornstarch paste, blend all well and heat through. Serve over rice.

CHINESE PORK
[Serves 4]

2 tablespoons peanut or salad oil	¼ cup sliced green onions
1 cup diced or slivered cooked pork	1 can condensed cream of vegetable soup
½ cup sliced celery	¼ cup water
½ cup cooked bean sprouts	2 teaspoons soy sauce
½ cup sliced mushrooms	2 cups torn spinach leaves
	Chow mein noodles

Heat oil in blazer pan over high heat, cook pork, celery, bean sprouts, mushrooms and green onions until meat is browned and vegetables are just tender.

Reduce heat to simmer and blend in soup, water, soy sauce and spinach. Heat, stirring now and then. When heated through, serve over noodles.

HANDY HAM SUPPER
[Serves 4 to 6]

1 pound ground beef	1 egg
1 4½-ounce can deviled ham	2 or 3 tablespoons butter or margarine
½ cup corn flake crumbs	1 package dry mushroom soup
1½ cups milk	
1 cup water	

Mix ground beef, deviled ham, crumbs, ½ cup of the milk and egg; form into small balls.

Sauté in butter in large blazer pan; remove and keep warm.

Blend dry mushroom soup into pan drippings; gradually stir in water and remaining cup milk. Cook until sauce thickens and comes to boil. Return meat balls to sauce; cover; simmer 10 minutes or more to blend flavors.

HAMHASH
[Serves 4]

3 tablespoons butter or margarine	2 cups cooked, chopped ham
2 cups cooked and diced potatoes	1 cup sour cream
Fine-cut chives	Salt and fresh-ground pepper

Melt butter in blazer pan over direct heat and lightly sauté potatoes and ham. Add sour cream and season to taste. Mix gently.

Place pan over hot water and stir slowly until potatoes and ham are very hot. Sprinkle with chives and serve immediately.

HAM OR TONGUE STROGANOFF
[Serves 6]

3 tablespoons shortening	⅛ teaspoon powdered marjoram
1 cup thin-sliced onions	1 3-ounce can sliced mushrooms
2 cups diced cooked ham or tongue	1 tablespoon cornstarch
1 teaspoon salt	2 tablespoons dry sherry or dry vermouth
1 teaspoon dry mustard	2 tablespoons catsup
⅛ teaspoon fresh-cracked pepper	
½ cup sour cream	

Melt shortening in large blazer pan over direct heat. Add onions and cook 5 minutes, stirring frequently. Add ham or tongue, salt, mustard, pepper, marjoram and mushrooms and cook, covered, 5 minutes.

Blend cornstarch and sherry and add to pan, stirring constantly until thick.

Blend catsup and sour cream and add, stirring to mix thoroughly. Serve over hot noodles or rice.

A VARIETY OF MEATS
IN A VARIETY OF WAYS

First, one of my initial recipe creations, dreamed up for the Lum and Abner radio show about 25 years ago.

THE ORIGINAL LUMBURGER
[Serves 1]

1 tablespoon butter	thick
1 patty ground steak, 3¾	1 egg
inches across, ½ inch	Seasonings to taste

Melt butter in blazer pan. Cut 1½-inch circle out of meat patty, leaving a ring. (Reserve circle of meat for next one.) Cook ring of meat in butter for 30 seconds; break egg carefully into hole so it stays whole. Cook, turning once, to desired doneness. Seasoning can be over or mixed in with meat. When done, place in sesame hamburger roll or any likely bread.

PTOMAINE TOMMY'S EGG ROYAL
[Serves 1]

¼ pound ground sirloin	½ cup coarsely chopped
1 egg	onions (optional)
Salt and pepper	1 cup mild chili con carne
Butter	with kidney beans

Mix meat and egg well, season with salt and pepper, form into patty and fry in butter on both sides. If onions are used, fry them with the patty. Garnish with chili con carne.

DELUXEBURGERS
[Serves 4]

1 pound ground round steak	1 tablespoon butter
1 tablespoon A.1. sauce	4 slices jellied cranberry sauce
1 tablespoon minced onion	Pineapple-Curry Sauce (see
1 teaspoon salt	below)

Combine beef, A.1. sauce, onion and salt; toss lightly and shape into 4 patties. In blazer pan over medium heat, fry to desired doneness.

Top each hamburger patty with slice of cranberry sauce and divide Pineapple-Curry Sauce over all.

PINEAPPLE-CURRY SAUCE

1 9-ounce can crushed pine-	1 tablespoon butter
apple	1 teaspoon curry powder

Combine pineapple, butter and curry and heat gently.

HAMBURGER PAUL GETTY
[Serves 4]

2 pounds ground beef	Breadcrumbs
Salt, pepper and nutmeg	3 tablespoons butter
1 tablespoon minced onion	4 tablespoons crisp onions,
1 egg	fried in butter
2 egg yolks, beaten	

Season meat with salt, fresh-crushed pepper and nutmeg. Work in the onion and raw egg. Mold into a flat, oval shape; dip into egg yolks and coat well; then roll in breadcrumbs.

Sauté hamburger in butter in blazer pan over high

heat to required doneness. Remove from pan and serve, topped with onions.

JIFFY HAMBURGERS
[Serves 4 to 6]

1½ pounds ground beef
2 tablespoons A.1. sauce
6 strips bacon

1 teaspoon salt, or seasoned or smoked salt

Blend beef with A.1. sauce and salt. Shape into 6 large patties. Wrap each patty with strip of bacon. Pan broil until bacon is crisp and meat is done to taste.

SLOPPY MOP-UPS
[Serves 8]

1 egg, slightly beaten
½ cup Italian seasoned dry breadcrumbs
¾ teaspoon salt
¼ teaspoon Tabasco sauce
1 pound ground beef
Flour

2 to 4 tablespoons butter or margarine
2 8-ounce cans tomato sauce with cheese
½ pound small cocktail frankfurters
1 loaf French bread

Combine egg, breadcrumbs, salt and Tabasco in large bowl. Mix in beef and form into 16 small meat balls. Dredge with flour and place in refrigerator until ready to use.

Melt 2 tablespoons butter in blazer pan over direct flame. Add half the meat balls and brown well, turning often. Remove from pan and keep warm while browning remaining meat balls, adding butter if necessary. Return other meat balls to pan and pour tomato sauce over all; add frankfurters. Cover and simmer 10 minutes.

Meanwhile cut French bread in half, lengthwise, then into four pieces each, crosswise. Divide meat and sauce over the 8 pieces of bread and serve, open-sandwich style.

One of the culinary attractions of Southern California is the Scandia Restaurant in West Hollywood.

SCANDIA'S SCANDINAVIAN MEAT BALLS
[Serves 4]

½ pound ground beef or veal
½ pound ground pork
½ cup fresh breadbrumbs
1 cup milk
Butter
½ cup chopped onions
1 egg, beaten
1 teaspoon salt

¼ teaspoon fresh-ground
    pepper
Pinch allspice
Oil or clarified butter
1 tablespoon flour
½ cup broth, consommé or
    milk

Combine ground meats and grind once more, together. Soak breadcrumbs in ½ cup of the milk.

In small amount of butter, sauté onions until tender but not browned.

Combine meat, crumbs, onion, egg, salt, pepper and allspice in a mixing bowl. Beat at low speed in mixer, or with wire whip, while adding remaining ½ cup of milk, which has been heated to lukewarm. This makes a sloppy mixture, so put in refrigerator until it is firm enough to be formed into bite-size meat balls.

Fry them in oil or clarified butter until browned on all sides. Drain off fat. Dredge meat balls with flour from a sifter. Add broth and cook and stir 3 minutes. Reduce heat to simmer and cook until sauce is thickened. Add salt and pepper to taste.

VIENNESE MEAT BALLS
[Makes about 25]

½ cup pork sausage
2 cups cooked and ground
    veal
2 eggs
4 anchovy filets or 1 heaping
    teaspoon anchovy paste
1 cup sour cream

1 teaspoon fine-chopped
    parsley
Fresh-ground pepper to
    taste
6 tablespoons butter or
    margarine
Cornstarch

Sauté sausage, breaking up into pieces. Mix together very thoroughly, the sausage, veal, eggs, well-chopped anchovy filets, or paste, and parsley. Season with pepper. Form into small balls and coat with or roll in cornstarch.

Melt butter in blazer pan and brown meat balls over Sterno heat. Spear with wood toothpicks and serve with sour cream on the side, for dipping.

BARBECUED FRANKFURTER DISH
[Serves 4 to 5]

2 tablespoons butter or margarine	1 tablespoon molasses
1 pound frankfurters	1 teaspoon prepared mustard
½ cup chopped onion	½ teaspoon vinegar
1 can condensed tomato rice soup	½ teaspoon Worcestershire sauce
½ soup can water	4 drops Tabasco sauce

Melt butter in blazer pan over medium heat, add franks and onion and cook until onion is tender and franks browned on all sides.

Add soup, water, molasses, mustard, vinegar, Worcestershire and Tabasco and simmer 15 minutes, stirring often.

Serve on hot plates or on frankfurter buns with sauce over. At about 7 franks to the pound, either add 1 more and serve 2 per plate, or 1 with 3 seconds.

EMINCE OF CALF'S LIVER DELMONICO
[Serves 4]

¼ cup (½ stick) butter	2 tablespoons flour
1 pound calf's liver, julienned	2 tablespoons white vinegar
Salt and pepper	½ cup white wine
½ onion, minced	1½ cups brown sauce or beef gravy
¼ pound mushrooms, sliced	

Heat butter in blazer pan; add liver, seasoned with salt and pepper, plus onion and mushrooms; brown. Add flour and mix well. Add vinegar, wine and brown sauce. Bring to gentle boil and serve immediately.

Care must be taken not to cook too long or liver will be tough.

VEAL KIDNEYS FLAMBE ALLA EXCELSIOR, ROME
[Serves 6]

3 pounds veal kidneys
1/4 cup flour
1 teaspoon salt
1/4 teaspoon pepper

4 tablespoons olive oil
1 tablespoon parsley
1/2 clove garlic, minced
3 drops Tabasco sauce

3 tablespoons brandy, warmed

Remove membranes and connective tissue from kidneys. Wash and drain well. Cut into thin slices. Shake up flour, salt and pepper in a bag; add kidney slices and shake to coat well.

Heat oil, parsley and garlic in blazer pan over strong direct heat. Add kidney slices and Tabasco and sauté until brown all over, 8 to 10 minutes. Cover and simmer 3 minutes. Uncover, add brandy and set ablaze. Serve very hot on fluffy rice.

TONGUE WITH PLUM SAUCE
[Serves 4]

3/4 cup plum jam
1 tablespoon wine vinegar
2 tablespoons red wine

Pinch powdered cloves
8 slices cooked tongue,
1/4-inch thick

Combine first four ingredients and heat in blazer pan over boiling water, blending well. Serve over hot tongue, 2 slices or more per serving.

TONGUE JUBILEE
[Serves 4]

¾ cup cherry jam
¼ cup Port wine
Pinch rosemary

8 or 12 slices cooked tongue,
¼-inch thick

Combine jam, wine and rosemary and heat through in blazer pan, blending thoroughly. Either heat tongue slices in sauce, or serve sauce over tongue.

TONGUE BIGARADE
[Serves 4]

¼ cup water
1 6-ounce can concentrated
frozen orange juice
1 tablespoon lemon juice

2 tablespoons cornstarch
2 tablespoons water
8 or 12 slices cooked tongue,
¼-inch thick

Heat water and juices in blazer pan.

Blend together cornstarch and the 2 tablespoons of water and add to juices. Bring to a boil, stirring constantly.

Reduce heat, add tongue and cover, cooking until meat is heated through.

Did you know that cranberries were originally called craneberries by the Pilgrims, because they were the favorite food of the cranes that abounded in Massachusetts Colony? Somewhere that first "e" got lost.

CRANBERRY TONGUE
[Serves 4]

¾ cup whole cranberry
sauce
⅛ teaspoon allspice

¼ cup apricot nectar
12 slices cooked tongue,
¼-inch thick

Put cranberries, allspice and nectar into blazer pan over boiling water and heat, stirring until well blended.

Either add tongue and heat through or serve sauce over hot sliced tongue.

TONGUE WITH ORANGE OR APRICOT SAUCE
[Serves 4]

¾ cup orange marmalade or apricot jam
2 tablespoons lemon juice

½ teaspoon powdered sugar
8 or 12 ¼-inch slices cooked tongue

Prepare as any of the tongue recipes above.

SAUCY TONGUE
[Serves 4]

12 slices cooked tongue, ¼-inch thick
1 green pepper
4 slices canned pineapple
2 cups canned pineapple juice

¼ cup sugar
¼ teaspoon garlic salt
¼ cup vinegar
¼ cup water
4 tablespoons cornstarch
Cooked rice

Cut tongue slices in julienne strips; cut green pepper in small diamonds; cut pineapple slices into 4 pieces each.

In blazer pan over direct high heat, place pineapple juice, sugar, garlic salt, and vinegar and bring to a boil. Add tongue, pineapple and green pepper and bring to boil again. Blend well.

Blend together cornstarch and water. Add to blazer pan; cook 4 minutes, stirring constantly, until sauce thickens. Serve over hot, cooked rice.

CHOP SUSIE
[Serves 6]

2 tablespoons butter or
    margarine
1 pound ground beef
1/2 cup chopped onion
2 tablespoons A.1. sauce
1 teaspoon salt

1 4-ounce can sliced
    mushrooms, drained
1 No. 2 1/2 can tomatoes
    (3 1/2 cups)
2 cups cooked elbow or shell
    macaroni

Melt butter in blazer pan over medium heat. Add beef, onion, A.1. sauce, salt and mushrooms. Sauté 10 minutes. Add tomatoes and macaroni, blend well and heat thoroughly.

With this serve green salad, crisp noodles and fresh fruit dessert.

This is a favorite dish that Mary Healy feeds her husband, Peter Lind Hayes.

MARY HEALY'S CHILI CON CARNE
[Serves 6]

3 pounds round or chuck
    steak
3 tablespoons flour
2 teaspoons salt
1/2 teaspoon fresh-ground
    pepper
3 tablespoons butter
3 cloves garlic
3 cups chopped onions

2 cups canned stewed
    tomatoes
4 slices bacon in 1-inch
    pieces
5 tablespoons chili powder
2 cups canned chili beans
3 tablespoons grated
    Parmesan cheese
1/4 cup chopped parsley

Cut steak into 1-inch cubes; toss in mixing bowl with flour, salt and pepper.

Melt butter in heavy enameled saucepan. Add meat and garlic and brown meat lightly on all sides. Add onions and sauté gently until they are transparent. Add tomatoes and bacon pieces, then barely cover meat with water.

Separately, mix chili powder into a paste with a little

water, then add to saucepan. Simmer contents over low heat, uncovered, for 3 hours, adding a little water occasionally as necessary to keep moist.

Remove pan from heat and let stand, covered, overnight—but not in refrigerator.

Before serving return pot to heat and bring to simmer and let simmer 30 minutes, stirring in beans just before placing in chafing dish. Garnish with cheese and top with parsley. Keep warm over hot water.

Vegetables in Chafing Dishes

PEAS WITH PROSCIUTTO
[Serves 4]

3 cups tender, young peas
¼ cup butter
½ cup chopped prosciutto
   (or Smithfield ham)

1 teaspoon sugar
Fresh-ground pepper
¼ cup water in which peas
   were cooked

Boil peas in smallest quantity unsalted water. Reserve ¼ cup of liquid when draining peas.

In blazer pan, melt butter, then sauté prosciutto over low heat. Do not let butter brown. Add peas, sugar, pepper and water from peas. Simmer slowly 5 minutes. Taste and salt if needed. Serve. (In Italy this is served as separate course.)

YOUNG PEAS FLORENTINE
[Serves 4]

2 pounds fresh green peas in
   pods
½ cup olive oil
¼ pound diced cooked ham
1 cup water
1 tablespoon finely chopped

parsley
1 garlic clove, on toothpick
⅛ teaspoon baking soda
Salt and pepper
1 cup cooked chopped
   spinach

Shell peas. Put olive oil in blazer pan, add peas, ham, water, parsley, garlic, baking soda, salt and pepper. Bring to boil over high heat. Adjust flame to lower heat and simmer mixture until peas are tender.

Remove garlic, stir in cooked spinach and serve immediately.

PEAS-ON-THE-SIDE
[Serves 4]

2½ tablespoons butter
2 tablespoons water
1 cup thin-sliced
    mushrooms

2 cups fresh peas (or 2
    10-ounce packages
    frozen)
1 small onion, thin-sliced
¼ teaspoon salt

Melt butter in blazer pan; add the other ingredients. Cover tightly and cook over moderate heat, shaking the pan occasionally to prevent sticking.

Cook fresh peas until tender—8 to 20 minutes. For frozen peas, start timing when steam begins to escape, and cook 5 to 10 minutes.

HONG KONG PEA PODS
[Serves 4]

4 cloves garlic, crushed
3 tablespoons lard
½ cup pork loin in small
    cubes
4 tablespoons chopped
    shrimp

Soy sauce and fresh-crushed
    pepper to taste
3 cups washed and trimmed
    pea pods (snow peas)
1 teaspoon sugar

Brown garlic in hot lard in blazer pan over high heat; add pork and cook well, stirring for about 10 minutes or until pork cubes are done. Add shrimp, sugar, soy sauce and pepper and blend well. Add peas and stir over high heat until crisp, about 3 minutes.

If you want peas cooked more well done, cover pan and steam about 3 minutes.

This is a recipe that Mary Lee Westcoat of Uniontown, Pa., created and was good enough to send me.

GREENS AND MUSHROOMS
[Serves 6 to 8]

1 package frozen collard greens
Salt and pepper to taste
1 package frozen chopped spinach
2 cups sour cream
½ teaspoon onion salt
Dash lemon juice
1 cup bacon bits
1 cup mushrooms sautéed in butter

Cook collard greens in 1½ cups of water with salt and pepper for 1 hour. Add spinach, onion salt and lemon juice and cook 10 minutes longer. Add bacon bits and mushrooms and mix in sour cream. Simmer slowly 10 minutes more.

Transfer to chafing dish blazer pan and keep warm over hot water.

SHERRIED MUSHROOMS
[Serves 4]

3 tablespoons butter
1 pound fresh mushrooms washed, drained and stemmed
1 tablespoon flour
1 chicken bouillon cube
¼ cup dry white wine, heated
1 bay leaf
Dash nutmeg
2 tablespoons sherry

Heat butter in blazer pan of electric chafing dish at high. Add mushrooms and flour. Toss mushrooms while sautéeing lightly.

Dissolve bouillon cube in white wine, pour over mushrooms, add bay leaf and nutmeg and continue cooking at medium, uncovered, for 6 minutes, stirring occasionally. Add sherry and place over hot water bath to keep warm during serving. Set control at low to maintain slight bubbling.

CHEESE AND ONIONS
[Serves 4 to 6]

2 tablespoons butter
4 mild onions, sliced thin
1 tablespoon flour
¾ teaspoon salt
1 teaspoon prepared mustard
1 teaspoon A.1. sauce

½ teaspoon paprika
Dash pepper
2 drops Tabasco sauce
¾ pound Cheddar cheese, shredded
1 tall can evaporated milk

Melt butter in blazer pan over direct heat and cook onions until limp. Blend in flour, salt, mustard, A.1., paprika, pepper and Tabasco. Add cheese and milk a little at a time and heat until cheese melts and mixture bubbles, stirring occasionally.

Place pan over boiling water, cover and cook until onions are tender. Serve on toast.

CORN SUPREME
[Makes 1 cup]

Fresh corn on the cob

For 1 cup cooked kernels

½ cup cream
½ teaspoon sugar
¼ teaspoon salt
¼ teaspoon fresh-ground pepper

Husk corn, drop whole ears into boiling salted water. Let come to boil again and cook 4 minutes. Remove and plunge into cold water until cool. Cut kernels from cob by splitting down center of each row, then scraping and cutting from cob.

Measure kernels and to each cup, add ½ cup cream, ½ teaspoon sugar, and pepper and salt to taste. Mix well in blazer pan, bring to boil, lower heat and simmer until thick, 3 to 5 minutes, stirring constantly to prevent sticking.

CORN FRITTERS
[Serves 4 to 6]

3 eggs, separated	½ teaspoon salt
1⅔ cups cooked or canned	⅛ teaspoon pepper
whole kernel corn	¼ cup sifted all-purpose flour
	Butter

Beat egg yolks until thick and fluffy. Blend in corn, salt and pepper. Add flour and blend well.

Whip egg whites until stiff. Fold into corn mixture.

Heat blazer pan over direct flame and melt 1 tablespoon butter in it. Drop fritter mixture by tablespoons and brown on both sides, about 3 minutes. Remove fritters to warm serving dish, wipe pan with paper towel, rebutter and repeat.

Serve fritters hot with butter, syrup or confectioners' sugar. Or as an accompaniment to chicken, roast meat or fish.

Rösti is a Swiss specialty and can be a meal in itself.

ROSTI
[Serves 2 to 4]

1 pound potatoes, boiled in	½ pound butter
jackets	½ pound chopped onions
	Salt and pepper to taste

Peel potatoes and cut into small cubes or into Shoestrings.

Melt ¼ pound of butter in blazer pan until about to sizzle. Add potatoes and onions and mix well. When vegetables have absorbed butter, add remainder of butter and continue frying until golden.

Using pancake turner or a plate that fits inside the pan, press the potatoes down as flat as possible while a golden crust forms.

Remove and serve piping hot.

ZUCCHINI SALMAGUNDI
[Serves 6]

6 zucchinis or equal amount
   of summer squash
3 tablespoons butter
1 clove garlic, mashed
   (optional)
1 tablespoon chopped onions

2 green peppers, chopped
   fine
¾ cup milk
1 cup corn kernels
½ cup grated Cheddar cheese
2 teaspoons salt

Trim squash and cut into dice.

Melt butter in blazer pan over boiling water, add garlic, onions, peppers and squash and fry until tender, stirring constantly.

Add milk, corn, cheese and salt, mix well and cook over water another 10 minutes.

Main Dishes for all Occasions

HAM AND EGG SHORTCAKE
[Serves 4]

½ cup chopped green pepper
2 tablespoons butter
1 can cream of mushroom
  soup
¼ cup chopped pimiento
½ teaspoon salt

¼ teaspoon nutmeg
Pinch pepper
4 hard-cooked eggs, cut in
  thick slices
4 1-ounce slices boiled ham
4 hot cornbread squares

Cook green pepper in butter in blazer pan until tender.
Add soup, pimiento, and seasonings; blend eggs in, stirring carefully to avoid breaking slices. Heat thoroughly.

Put a slice of ham on each cornbread square. Divide
creamed egg mixture over squares. Serve with broccoli and
a salad of sliced cucumbers in vinegar.

ASPARAGUS PANCAKE
[Serves 1]

3 medium or 4 small stalks
  cooked or canned
  asparagus

1 egg
2 dashes celery salt
Butter

Put first 3 ingredients in blender, turn to high speed
until contents become smooth and creamy—2 to 3 minutes. Pour in buttered blazer pan, cook one side until
done, turn over carefully. When done, serve on warmed
plate.

MISSION INN SCRAMBLED EGGS
[Serves 2]

3 eggs
3 tablespoons heavy cream
Salt to taste
3 ounces butter
6 chicken livers, blanched in milk
3 large mushrooms, sliced

1 tablespoon minced chives
1/4 teaspoon basil
3 tablespoons Burgundy wine
1/2 cup brown sauce or beef gravy

Beat eggs in small mixing bowl with cream and salt.

Heat 2 ounces of the butter in blazer pan of chafing dish; add livers, then mushrooms and sauté until well browned. Add chives and basil and sauté 1 minute longer. Add wine and brown sauce mixed together, and cook until sauce is reduced by 1/3.

In another pan heat remaining butter and scramble the eggs, stirring lightly while shaking pan until eggs reach the soft stage.

Put eggs on heated serving plate in neat mound. Arrange chicken livers and mushrooms with sauce around eggs. Serve at once.

LOX AND EGGS
[Serves 1]

3 tablespoons chopped onion
1 tablespoon butter
2 eggs

1 large slice lox (salted smoked salmon), diced
Dash black pepper
1/2 teaspoon chopped parsley

Sauté onion in hot butter in blazer pan until transparent but not brown; add lox and stir gently until golden.

Beat eggs and pour into pan, sprinkle with pepper and stir gently. When eggs are set to desired consistency, sprinkle a benediction of parsley over, transfer to warm plate and serve.

DRIED BEEF WITH EGGS
[Serves 4]

4 ounces dried beef (1
    package)
2½ tablespoons butter

6 eggs
6 tablespoons cream
Celery salt

Cut dried beef into 1-inch squares with kitchen shears. Melt butter in blazer pan, fry beef for 3 minutes, stirring.

Beat eggs and cream slightly; pour over beef; season with celery salt, stir gently while cooking. Serve immediately, while hot and moist.

SAVORY EGG PANCAKE
[Serves 4 to 6]

2 medium potatoes
5 tablespoons butter
6 eggs

Pinch salt
3 ounces Gruyère cheese,
    diced

2 tablespoons heavy cream

Peel, dry and slice potatoes thin. Heat 3 tablespoons of the butter in blazer pan, add potatoes and cook over low heat until lightly golden on both sides. Remove and keep hot.

Beat eggs well with salt; add cheese, cream, then potatoes. Cook in pan with balance of butter, stirring occasionally. Serve hot.

CHINESE SCRAMBLED EGGS
[Serves 4]

¼ pound sausage, bulk or
    link, in small pieces
½ cup sliced celery
⅓ cup fresh or canned bean
    sprouts, drained

4 eggs, beaten
¼ cup milk
¼ teaspoon salt
Pinch pepper

Brown sausage lightly in blazer pan. Pour off excess fat; add celery, cook 2 to 3 minutes; add bean sprouts.

Combine eggs, milk, salt, and pepper. Pour over sausage mixture.

Cook over low heat, stirring occasionally, until eggs are set but vegetables are still slightly crisp, about 10 minutes.

OYSTER-AVOCADO OMELET
[Serves 4]

6 eggs, lightly beaten
2 tablespoons water
½ teaspoon salt
⅛ teaspoon fresh-ground
   black pepper
1 teaspoon Worcestershire

sauce
1 dozen fresh oysters or
   frozen, thawed
½ cup dry breadcrumbs
¼ cup melted butter
1 avocado, peeled and cubed

Combine eggs, water, salt, pepper and Worcestershire. Dip oysters in the mixture, then in crumbs and sauté in butter in blazer pan until lightly browned.

Add remaining egg mixture and avocado to oysters and cook as an omelet, lifting egg from pan edges as it cooks. When set, fold, omelet style, and serve.

CRABMEAT NEWBERG
[Serves 2]

2 tablespoons butter
2 tablespoons flour
1⅓ cups light cream
3 egg yolks, beaten slightly
1 teaspoon lemon juice

Salt
1 cup flaked crabmeat
3 tablespoons sherry
   (optional)

In top pan of chafing dish over direct low flame, melt butter. Blend in flour. Add cream, cook and stir until sauce begins to thicken.

Blend a few tablespoons of the hot sauce into egg yolks, then pour back into the hot sauce, stirring constantly.

Adjust flame to medium, continue to cook and stir sauce until thick. Add salt to taste. Stir in crabmeat, sherry and lemon juice. Cook just long enough to heat through.

Serve at once in pastry shells, over hot toast or in a split popover.

FINNAN HADDIE BRUNCH
[Serves 4]

1½ pounds finnan haddie	Paprika to taste
4 tablespoons butter	⅛ teaspoon cayenne pepper
4 tablespoons flour	Hot waffle squares
2 cups milk	

Poach fish by placing in cold water to cover and heating to just below boiling, cooking until it can be flaked easily, about 5 minutes. Drain and flake.

In blazer pan over medium heat, melt butter, add flour and cook until it bubbles.

Place blazer pan over hot water pan and stir in milk. Cook, stirring once in a while, until sauce is thickened. Season with paprika and cayenne and add cooked fish. Heat through. Serve over waffles.

BEEF WITH TOMATOES AND GREEN PEPPERS
[Serves 4]

3 tablespoons oil	3 green peppers, cut in wedges
1 pound tenderloin or filet beef, sliced thin	3 tomatoes, quartered
1 teaspoon salt	1 chicken bouillon cube dissolved in 1 cup hot water
⅛ teaspoon pepper	
1 scallion, cut into ½-inch pieces	2 teaspoons cornstarch
1 clove garlic, minced	¼ cup water
1 teaspoon soy sauce	

In top pan of chafing dish, over direct high flame, heat oil until it is very hot. Add beef slices, salt and pepper. Sauté 1 minute, stirring constantly. Add scallion, garlic, green peppers, tomatoes.

Reduce flame to medium, slowly add chicken stock. Cook 2 minutes, stirring occasionally. Cover, turn flame to low, simmer gently 10 minutes.

Add cornstarch mixed with water and soy sauce, stirring constantly until mixture is smooth and thick.

Serve with hot rice.

HASH WITH EGGS
[Serves 4]

2 cups cubed roast or corned beef
2 cups diced cooked potatoes
1/4 cup minced green pepper or onion
2 tablespoons minced

parsley
2 tablespoons A.1. sauce
Salt and fresh-ground pepper to taste
2 tablespoons butter
4 poached eggs

Blend all ingredients except butter and eggs well.

Melt butter in blazer pan over medium heat. Add hash and brown, then turn and brown other side. Press down with pancake turner to form crust. Divide into 4 servings, top each with a poached egg and serve immediately.

MAIN DISH DELUXEBURGERS
[Serves 4]

2 pounds ground round
1 1/4 cups Burgundy
Salt and pepper to taste
1 tablespoon minced parsley
3 tablespoons butter or margarine

1 6-ounce can sliced mushrooms with liquid
4 split, toasted, buttered hamburger rolls
8 large slices raw or French-fried onions

Using your hands, mix ground round and 1/4 cup of the wine together. Add seasonings and parsley and mix well. Form into 8 1/4-pound burgers.

Melt butter in blazer pan until it sizzles. Brown hamburgers on both sides quickly. Add mushrooms and mushroom liquid and rest of wine; simmer, uncovered, 8 to 10 minutes, basting sauce over meat several times.

When done to taste, place patty on each ½ roll, decorate with raw onion slice or hot French fried onions. Divide sauce over all.

SALTIMBOCCA, OR JUMP-IN-THE-MOUTH
[Serves 6]

12 ¼-pound veal scallops
1¼ teaspoons salt
¼ teaspoon ground black
    pepper

½ teaspoon dried sage
12 slices prosciutto ham
4 tablespoons butter
¼ cup Marsala wine

Season veal pieces with salt and pepper and sage, then cover each piece of veal with a slice of ham, cut to same size. Fasten with toothpicks.

Sauté veal in butter in blazer pan over high heat on each side for 2 minutes. Add wine and reduce heat; cook until veal is tender. Place on a heated serving dish, ham side up. Remove toothpicks. Pour pan sauce over all.

PACIFIC PALISADES VEAL
[Serves 4]

2 tablespoons butter or
    margarine
3 tablespoons fine-chopped
    green or sweet red
    pepper
1½ tablespoons flour

1 cup chicken broth
Salt and pepper
1½ tablespoons currant jelly
½ teaspoon powdered
    rosemary
8 thin slices cold roast veal

Heat butter in blazer pan over medium heat; add green pepper and cook 3 minutes, stirring. Stir in flour and let bubble. Add chicken broth and stir until mixture boils and is thickened. Season to taste, then blend in jelly and rosemary.

Place pan over hot water and lay veal in sauce and cook until meat is heated through.

ONE-DISH LUNCHEON RABBIT
[Serves 4]

¼ cup butter or margarine
½ cup fine-cut green pepper
½ cup fine-cut celery
1 4-ounce can sliced
    mushrooms, drained
¼ cup flour
1 tablespoon dry mustard

½ teaspoon salt
Pinch cayenne
1 pint stale beer or ale
4 cups grated sharp Cheddar
    cheese
4 split, toasted and buttered
    English muffins

Melt butter in large blazer pan over direct heat, add green pepper, celery and mushrooms and sauté until pepper and celery are soft, about 8 minutes.

Stir in flour, mustard, salt and cayenne. Gradually mix in the beer, stirring until smooth and slightly thickened. Add the grated Cheddar and stir with a wooden spoon until blended smooth and heated through.

Divide among 8 muffin halves on 4 warm plates.

MELTED CHEESE WITH SMOKED TURKEY
[Serves 4]

2 cups Basic Welsh Rabbit
    (see Index)
4 English muffins, split and

toasted
⅔ cup smoked turkey,
    julienned

Keeping the serving plates very hot is the secret of this sort of dish.

Heat the Welsh Rabbit. Place half a muffin on very hot service plate. Alongside put some turkey. Cover muffin with hot rabbit; top with second half of muffin and top that with more rabbit. Serve at once with fork and knife.

TURKEY-STUFFED CREPES
[Serves 6]

Crêpes

3 eggs	2 tablespoons melted butter
1 cup milk	or margarine

1 cup pancake mix

Mix all ingredients in blender to thickness of cream. Let stand overnight.

Filling

1 can condensed cream of	3 cups diced cooked turkey
mushroom soup	¼ cup cream

Combine all ingredients and heat, stirring often.

Method: Heat blazer pan and grease with butter lightly. Pour in ¼ cup crêpe batter and tilt pan to spread evenly. When bottom browns turn over. Stack the pancakes and keep warm.

Spoon ½ cup turkey filling on center of each crêpe and roll. Serve with slice of cranberry sauce and/or hot turkey gravy.

CHINESE ALMOND CHICKEN
[Serves 4]

¼ cup salad oil	sliced
2 raw chicken breasts, thinly	½ cup blanched almonds
sliced (about 2 cups)	2 tablespoons soy sauce
2 cups diced celery	3 cups chicken broth
2 cups canned diced bamboo	¼ cup cornstarch
shoots	½ cup water
1 can (5 ounces) water	¼ cup slivered toasted
chestnuts, drained and	almonds

In top pan of chafing dish, over direct high flame, heat oil. Add chicken and fry for a few minutes. Add remaining ingredients except cornstarch, water and slivered almonds. Mix well. Cover tightly and cook 5 minutes without disturbing.

Mix cornstarch and water and add to chicken mixture, stirring constantly. Reduce flame to medium, cook and stir until mixture thickens and is smooth. Add salt and pepper, if desired, sprinkle with slivered almonds and serve hot with fluffy or fried rice.

CREAMED CHICKEN WITH MUSHROOMS
[Serves 4 to 6]

2 tablespoons butter
2 tablespoons flour
1 cup chicken broth
1 teaspoon Worcestershire
   sauce
1 pimiento, cut in strips

½ cup cooked peas
12 large mushroom caps
¼ cup sherry
 2 cups cooked, diced chicken
   or turkey
¼ cup heavy cream
Salt and pepper

Melt butter in the top pan of chafing dish over direct low flame. Stir in flour, then chicken broth, stirring continuously until mixture thickens and becomes smooth. Add Worcestershire sauce, pimiento, peas, mushrooms and sherry. Simmer gently for 5 minutes, stirring occasionally. Add chicken or turkey and cream. Heat through, but do not boil. Season to taste. Serve on toast points or rice.

CHICKEN CURRY HASH
[Serves 4]

2 cups Curry Sauce (see
   Index)
1 cup heavy cream
1 slice pineapple, diced
1 medium tomato, peeled
   and diced

1 tablespoon chutney,
   fine-chopped
1 chicken breast, diced fine
1½ cups chicken dark meat,
   diced fine
2 cups steamed rice

Heat Curry Sauce and heavy cream in blazer pan. Add pineapple, tomato and chutney; blend well and bring to gentle boil. Add chicken and simmer over low heat 4 or 5 minutes.

Serve with rice.

DEVILED DRUMSTICKS
[Serves 4]

8 large chicken drumsticks	¼ teaspoon pepper or
⅓ cup flour	cayenne
1 teaspoon chili powder	6 tablespoons butter
1 teaspoon salt	1 cup chili sauce
3 drops Tabasco sauce	

Wash and dry drumsticks. Toss in paper bag with flour, chili powder, salt and pepper.

Brown drumsticks on all sides in skillet in 3 tablespoons of the butter for 12 minutes. Keep warm until ready to bring to table.

At table: Melt remaining 3 tablespoons butter in blazer pan over hot flame until sizzling. Add chicken legs and heat through for 5 minutes. Add chili sauce and Tabasco. Cover, reduce heat and simmer, turning drumsticks occasionally until tender, about 10 or 12 minutes. Serve 2 to a customer and spoon sauce over. Rice goes well with this dish.

FLAMING CHICKEN LIVERS
[Serves 4]

1 pound chicken livers, washed, drained and halved	1½ tablespoons minced green pepper or onion
Salt and fresh-ground pepper	1½ ounces brandy, warmed
2 tablespoons (¼ stick) butter or margarine	1 cup light cream
	2 tablespoons minced parsley or chives
	Hot egg noodles for 4

Sprinkle livers with salt and pepper to taste.

Melt butter in blazer pan over high heat. Reduce heat and add livers and green pepper. Sauté until light brown on all sides. Pour brandy over and flame. As soon as flame dies, blend in cream and continue stirring until sauce is slightly thick. Sprinkle with parsley (or chives if onion is not used above) and serve on hot noodles.

CHICKEN LIVERS GRECO
[Serves 4]

1 pound chicken livers	1 10-ounce package frozen
½ cup flour	green beans, cooked
1 teaspoon poultry seasoning	3 tablespoons crushed
Dash seasoned pepper	packaged stuffing mix
⅓ cup butter or margarine	2 tablespoons grated
1 cup chicken broth	Parmesan cheese

Cut livers in half and roll pieces in flour mixed with seasonings. Refrigerate until ready to use.

In top pan of chafing dish, melt butter over high flame. Add livers and sauté until lightly browned. Add broth and simmer over medium low flame for 5 minutes. Stir in cooked beans and simmer until heated through.

Combine stuffing mix and grated cheese, sprinkle over ingredients in pan; do not stir in. Cover pan, turn off flame and let stand a few minutes. Serve hot.

JULIENNE OF CALF'S LIVER
[Serves 4]

1½ pounds calf's liver in julienned strips

Marinade

1 cup French dressing	¼ teaspoon fresh-ground
1 tablespoon dry white wine	pepper
	½ teaspoon salt

½ cup flour	margarine
3 tablespoons butter or	1½ ounces brandy, heated
	Fluffy rice

Marinate liver strips in well-mixed marinade at room temperature at least 1 hour. Drain, and either dredge with flour or shake in bag with flour.

Melt butter in blazer pan until it is very hot, then sauté liver strips quickly on both sides until light brown, but do not overcook. Pour warm brandy over and flame. As soon as flame dies out, serve on individual portions of rice.

A specialty of Milan is known as Straw and Hay. It is served by Antonio Merlonghi, the maître d' at Le Gourmet Restaurant there, cooked from scratch at the table in a chafing dish fueled just as it is in the U.S.—by Sterno.

STRAW AND HAY
[Serves 6 as appetizer, 3 as main dish]

¼ cup butter or margarine
¾ cup heavy cream
2 ounces thin-sliced prosciutto or Virginia ham, cut in ½-inch strips
3 cups medium egg noodles, cooked
3 cups spinach-egg noodles, cooked
1 10-ounce package frozen tiny peas in butter sauce, cooked; or canned peas
1 teaspoon salt
Grated Parmesan cheese

Assemble all ingredients at table where they will be handy.

Melt butter in blazer pan of large chafing dish over medium heat. Stir in cream. Add ham, noodles, peas and salt. Toss with two forks to mix while heating well. Sprinkle with 2 tablespoons Parmesan; mix. Serve with additional Parmesan on side.

FETTUCCINE ALFREDO
[Serves 4]

1 pound noodles, barely cooked, and drained
1¼ cups soft, sweet butter
2 cups grated Parmesan
cheese
¾ cup heavy cream
1 egg yolk
Salt
Freshly ground pepper

Place noodles in top pan of chafing dish over direct low flame; add butter and Parmesan cheese; mix thoroughly and heat through, mixing constantly. Add heavy cream blended with egg yolk, sprinkle with salt and freshly ground black pepper. Toss with two forks to mix thoroughly.

GERMAN-STYLE POTATO SALAD
[Serves 8]

9 medium potatoes
½ pound bacon, diced
½ to ⅔ cup vinegar
1⅓ cups water

1½ tablespoons cornstarch
1 tablespoon white sugar
1½ teaspoons light brown
   sugar

Chopped parsley

Cook whole potatoes in jackets. When cooled, peel and slice. Set aside.

Put bacon into blazer pan of electric chafing dish and fry at high until golden and crisp. Drain on absorbent paper.

Mix vinegar, water, cornstarch and sugars and add to bacon drippings in blazer pan. Cook, stirring constantly, until thickened. Add sliced potatoes and heat through, stirring gently to coat potatoes. Garnish with parsley.

Place over hot water bath at medium setting to keep hot.

MONTE CRISTO SANDWICH
[Serves 1]

3 slices white sandwich bread
1 slice baked ham
1-ounce chicken slice
   Butter

1 slice Swiss cheese
1 egg
⅓ cup milk
   Cranberry sauce

Butter first slice of bread and cover with lean baked ham and chicken. Butter middle slice on both sides and place on meat. Cover with cheese. Add third slice of bread, buttered, over cheese. Trim crusts, cut sandwich in two, and secure with toothpicks. Beat egg and milk together well, and dip sandwich in mixture until coated on all sides.

Fry in butter on all sides until golden brown and crisp. Remove toothpicks and serve with cranberry sauce, a slice of jellied preferably.

CROQUE SENOR
[Serves 1]

1 slice Monterey Jack or Muenster cheese	crusts removed
1 slice Virginia or boiled ham	Sherry
2 slices sandwich bread,	Beaten egg
	Breadcrumbs
Olive oil	

Place slice of cheese and slice of ham, cut to fit, on 1 slice of bread. Cover with second slice and fasten together with toothpicks. Dip first in sherry, then in beaten egg, finally in breadcrumbs.

Fry in hot olive oil in blazer pan until golden brown on both sides and cheese begins to melt. Remove toothpicks, serve and eat at once.

TOASTED HAM AND MUSHROOM SANDWICHES
[Makes 4 to 6]

½ pound fresh mushrooms	3 tablespoons cream
1 tablespoon butter or margarine	1 cup ground cooked ham
1 tablespoon grated onion	8 to 12 slices bread
	Softened butter

Wash, drain and chop mushrooms fine. Sauté in blazer pan in 1 tablespoon butter for 2 minutes; add onion. When golden, add cream and ham and heat through, mixing well.

Remove from pan and spread mixture between slices of buttered bread; brush both sides of sandwich with soft butter, return sandwiches to pan and toast to golden brown on one side, turn with spatula or cake turner and toast other side.

Serve with cranberry sauce or jelly.

Drained canned mushrooms may be used instead of fresh.

How to Find a Happy Ending
with a Chafing Dish

Apple pie heated is twice as delicious as a cold slab. And heated apple pie with a ball of vanilla ice cream, flamed in rum, has got to be even more toothsome.

The same principle applies to heating and flaming such fruits as bananas, cherries, peaches—almost any your epicurean imagination can nominate.

And then we come to chafing dish–finished pancakes and crêpes!

This is where the skilled c.d. operator really shines, for starting with the popular Crêpes Suzette and continuing through the variations, here is a tasty roster of flaming flapjacks to bring any meal to a mouth-watering conclusion.

From Arnaud's Restaurant in the French quarter of New Orleans, comes this formula for making apple pie just about the greatest dessert to which I'm addicted.

APPLE PIE FLAMBEE
[Serves 6]

2 cups dark rum	Pinch ground cinnamon
6 whole cloves	1 hot apple pie
6 scoops vanilla ice cream	

Heat rum in chafing dish, add cloves and cinnamon.

Have pie divided into slices, on warm plates, each with a ball of ice cream.

Fire the rum and while it is blazing, divide it among the plates of pie and ice cream.

DRUNKEN APPLES
[Serves 4]

Juice from baked apples
⅔ cup Bourbon
3 tablespoons sugar

2 tablespoons lemon juice
4 Baked Apples (see below)
Cream

Pour juice or jelly from baked apples into blazer pan over moderate heat, adding ⅓ cup of the Bourbon, the sugar, and lemon juice. Stir until sugar is dissolved. Add baked apples and baste, heating until apples are warm.

Warm remaining ⅓ cup Bourbon, pour over apples and set ablaze. As soon as flames die serve with cream.

BAKED APPLES
[Serves 4]

4 baking apples
½ cup plumped raisins or
   currants

½ cup brown sugar
2 tablespoons butter
2 tablespoons water

Core apples and peel top half of each. Place in oven-proof dish or baking pan, fill centers with raisins, sprinkle sugar over, dot with butter and put water in bottom of pan. Bake in moderate (375°) oven until tender, 30 to 40 minutes. Keep at room temperature.

RUM-SOAKED APPLES
[Serves 6]

4 tart apples, peeled, cored
   and thin-sliced
Rum to cover
Flour
¼ cup (½ stick) butter

2 tablespoons high-proof
   rum, warmed
Powdered sugar and
   cinnamon, mixed

Soak apple slices in rum in tall, narrow bowl for 3 or 4 hours.

Drain, dry and dust with flour.

In blazer or crêpe pan, over direct flame, melt butter

and sauté apple slices until light brown on both sides. Add more butter if necessary.

Pour the warmed high-proof rum over and set afire. Serve on hot plates while still flaming, with sugar and cinnamon on the side.

FRUITS FLAMBE
[Makes about 3 cups]

1 No. 2 can pears, peaches, plums, or diced pineapple
4 drops each, almond and vanilla extract

1½ cups sugar
½ cup maraschino cherries
¼ cup warmed light rum

Spice bag

2 cinnamon sticks
6 cloves

Drain syrup from canned fruit into saucepan. Add sugar and spice bag. Simmer 20 minutes. Remove spice bag. Add extracts, canned fruit and cherries.

In top pan of chafing dish, over direct low flame, heat fruit mixture to just below the boiling point. Add warmed rum. Ignite. When flame dies, serve with vanilla ice cream.

FLAMING FRUIT COMPOTE
[Serves 6 to 8]

1½ pounds mixed dried fruit
1 cup sugar
1 tablespoon honey
Peel of ½ lemon cut into thin strips
Dash nutmeg

Cinnamon stick
3 tablespoons cornstarch
¾ cup Cointreau, Grand Marnier, or orange liqueur

Soak fruit overnight in enough cold water to cover it by an inch. Drain fruit in colander, reserving 1½ cups of liquid.

Pour liquid into blazer pan of electric chafing dish,

add sugar, honey, lemon peel and spices. Bring to a boil at high and continue cooking 15 minutes.

Mix cornstarch and ¼ cup Cointreau, add to syrup mixture, stirring constantly until slightly thickened. Add fruit and heat until bubbly.

To flame, heat ½ cup Cointreau, pour over fruit and ignite. Ladle flaming fruit into compote dishes or over individual servings of ice cream.

THE FLAMING BANANAS OF
THE BRONZE HORSE
[Serves 4]

4 tablespoons butter	5 bananas, halved both ways
½ cup sugar	½ cup warmed kirsch (or half
Peel from ½ lemon	kirsch and half dark
16 dates, pitted and	rum, warmed)
quartered, lengthwise	

Melt butter in wide chafing dish over high flame, add sugar and lemon zest (yellow part of skin) in strips, and dates. Cook until sugar begins to caramelize a light brown. Add bananas, stirring and turning pieces carefully until they are well warmed but not too soft. Pour warmed liqueur over, flame until alcohol is burned off, then serve at once, dividing sauce.

Variation: At the Excelsior Hotel in Rome, the sliced bananas are marinated in orange juice and 2 ounces of Curaçao for 1 hour before frying.

My cousins, the Jo Van Ronkels, sent me two glamorous desserts from California.

V. R.'S BANANAS FLAMBE
[Serves 4 to 6]

5 ounces (1¼ sticks) butter	8 ounces banana liqueur
6 unripe bananas, peeled	2 ounces 151-proof Puerto
Dark brown sugar	Rico rum, warmed
2 ounces Grand Marnier	

Melt butter in large, flat chafing dish or crêpe suzette pan and let it get hot.

Slice bananas in half lengthwise, and add to pan. Sprinkle generously with sugar. After bananas are hot, turn over and sprinkle other side with sugar. Add banana liqueur and Grand Marnier, mixing well with sauce. Before bananas get soft, pour in warmed rum and ignite. Let it burn and cook down until the sauce becomes slightly syrupy, by which time the bananas will be soft.

Serve bananas on warm plates, dividing sauce over.

CHERRIES JUBILEE A LA BEVERLY HILLS
[Serves 6]

2 1-pound (size 303) cans pitted black Bing cherries
2 teaspoons cornstarch
4 ounces Kijafa cherry wine
2 ounces cherry flavored brandy
1 ounce Grand Marnier
1 ounce fine cognac
2 ounces 151-proof Puerto Rico rum, warmed
6 scoops vanilla ice cream

Drain juice from cherries and over low heat thicken juice with cornstarch to a syrupy consistency, then add cherries again; warm.

Place in blazer pan and heat over direct flame. Add wine, brandy, Grand Marnier and cognac. Stir all together well and let cook 2 minutes. Add warmed rum, ignite and stir slightly with long-handled spoon.

Ladle cherries and sauce over vanilla ice cream in individual dishes.

FLAMING CHERRIES
[Serves 4]

1½ cups black pitted cherries
½ cup currant jelly
Juice of ½ orange
1 small piece lemon peel
½ bay leaf
½ cup Burgundy
1 ounce brandy or cognac, warmed
1 ounce Cointreau, warmed
4 scoops vanilla or cherry ice cream

Strain the juice off the cherries. Put cherries into chafing dish blazer pan. Add half the juice, the currant jelly, orange juice, lemon peel, bay leaf, and wine. Simmer about 15 minutes. While mixture is boiling briskly, add brandy and Cointreau. Ignite and mix with long-handled silver spoon, ladling liquid above the chafing dish so that it mixes with the air and the alcohol burns. As soon as flame dies out, serve over scoops of ice cream in individual dishes.

CHERRIES JUBILEE
[Serves 4 to 6]

2 No. 2 cans Bing or dark sweet cherries
¼ cup granulated sugar

1 tablespoon lemon juice
¼ cup light or dark rum, warmed

Drain off 1 cup juice from each can of cherries and reserve for other use.

Place remaining juice, sugar, cherries, and lemon juice in top pan of chafing dish over direct low heat. Stir gently, add warmed rum and heat through. Ignite. When flames die, serve alone or with vanilla or cherry ice cream.

A warning note from Mrs. Don Quinn of Hollywood:

"As to chafing dish cookery, an experience of Gail Patrick's some time ago touted me off ever experimenting with that.

"After serving a lovely dinner, Gail created Cherries Jubilee at the table. Her beautiful silver chafing dish made a stunning frame for the flaming masterpiece—until she caught the handle in her bracelet and flipped the whole concoction skyward.

"Such sophisticated and definitely 'in' arson you've never seen!

"Somehow, I was content to let well enough alone with no thought of trying to top her achievement."

From Charlotte Westberg, former head of the reference room at the N.Y. Public Library, now of Lausanne in Switzerland, comes this

EASY-BUT-ELEGANT PEACH FLAMBE
[Serves 4]

1 tablespoon butter	8 tablespoons mincemeat
Juice of 1 orange	3 ounces cognac, warmed
Lemon juice	Unsweetened whipped
Sugar	cream
1 large can peach halves with juice	

Melt butter in blazer pan of chafing dish. Add orange juice, a dash of lemon juice and sugar only if needed. Blend well, then add 1 cup of juice from peaches; heat to boiling point, then add peach halves and simmer until fruit is well heated.

Fill cavities of peach halves with mincemeat. Warm cognac, pour over and light. As soon as flames subside, serve peach halves and syrup, with the whipped cream on the side.

SPICED PEACHES
[Serves 4]

1 No. 2 can peach halves with juice	1 teaspoon grated lemon rind
1 tablespoon whole cloves	2-inch piece cinnamon stick
½ cup favorite jelly or preserves	Slivered almonds

Drain juice from peaches, reserve ½ cup. Pierce each peach half with a few cloves.

In top pan of chafing dish over low flame combine jelly or preserves with lemon rind and ½ cup peach juice. Cook until jelly melts. Add peaches and cinnamon stick. Simmer peach halves gently to heat through; remove to serving dishes.

Bring syrup to boil over moderate flame, cook and stir until thickened. Pour hot syrup over peaches.

Serve hot with a sprinkle of slivered almonds.

PINEAPPLE IN COGNAC CREAM
[Serves 6]

1 can chunk pineapple	3 ounces cognac
2 tablespoons sweet butter	4 ounces heavy cream

Drain pineapple well, reserving juice.

Melt butter in chafing dish pan; add pineapple chunks; stir and cook until lightly browned; add reserved juice and cognac. When mixture is hot, stir in cream. Continue heating, but do not let boil. Serve piping hot.

BRANDIED DATES
[Serves 4]

½ cup brandy	4 thin slices angel food,
1 teaspoon lemon juice	chiffon or sponge cake
24 dates stuffed with blanched almonds	1 cup heavy cream

Heat brandy and lemon juice in blazer pan over direct heat. Add dates, cover and simmer 8 minutes. For each serving, spoon 6 dates over cake slice placed on warm plate. Serve cream on the side.

This next recipe is somewhat similar to Zabaglione.

CUSTARD WITH CHARTREUSE
[Serves 4 to 6]

1 cup milk	2 tablespoons sugar
3 tablespoons yellow Chartreuse	6 egg yolks
	2 tablespoons cream

In blazer pan of small chafing dish over direct flame, heat milk, sugar and liqueur.

Meanwhile beat egg yolks with cream.

Pour hot milk mixture over eggs, stirring briskly. Return to chafing dish, this time over boiling water. Stir, cooking until custard will coat the spoon.

Strain into sherbet glasses and serve.

Which reminds me of a rather headstrong young man who was extricated from a rather dubious alliance by his father, who then sent the youth to Europe for his first visit.

The son, grateful, asked his father, just before he departed, if he had any advice to give him.

Papa pondered for a moment, then said:

"Yes, my boy. If you ever have your choice between green and yellow Chartreuse, always take the yellow."

APRICOT BETTY
[Serves 4]

4 tablespoons butter or margarine
3 tablespoons brown sugar
1/3 teaspoon ground cinnamon
2 1/2 cups small dry bread cubes

1 1-pound can apricots, sliced or chopped
1/2 teaspoon grated lemon peel
2 teaspoons lemon juice
Sprinkle ground nutmeg
Cream

In chafing dish blazer pan melt butter over direct heat; blend in sugar and cinnamon. Add cubes of bread and cook, tossing and stirring until browned. Stir in apricots, lemon peel and juice and cook until heated through, about 5 minutes more, stirring occasionally. Decorate with nutmeg and serve with cream.

DESSERT OMELET
[Serves 4]

1/2 cup sherry wine
1 cup raisins
3 eggs, separated
1 teaspoon salt

6 tablespoons sugar
2 cups cream
4 tablespoons cake flour
6 tablespoons butter

Heat wine and soak raisins until they are plump.

Beat egg yolks with salt, 2 tablespoons of the sugar, the cream and flour until well blended and smooth. Add wine and raisins and mix well.

Beat egg whites stiff, add remainder of sugar and beat 30 seconds more. Fold into other mixture and blend well.

Divide batter in half. Heat half the butter in blazer pan and cook half the batter like an omelet. Do not fold, but turn and cook until golden brown on both sides. Sprinkle with cinnamon and sugar; pull apart with forks for serving—immediately. Repeat with other half of batter.

This is a showmanly (and show-off) dish which should be climaxed with the lights out—or at least with only candlelight.

OMELET AU RHUM
[Serves 4]

6 eggs, lightly beaten
4 tablespoons water or
  milk
1½ tablespoons butter
  Sugar
½ cup warm rum

Add water or milk to eggs and beat lightly.

Melt butter in top of chafing dish over flame. When blazer pan is hot, add eggs, cooking quickly by raising edge and letting uncooked egg run under. When just set, sprinkle top lightly with sugar, and fold in half, using two forks.

Pour rum around omelet and ignite. (This is where the candlelight comes in.)

Ladle burning rum up and let it cascade back into pan a couple of times. Divide omelet after flames die, pouring sauce over.

CINNA-BERRY SAUCE
[Makes 1 cup]

1 cup fresh or frozen blueberries, thawed
3 tablespoons water
3 tablespoons sugar
¼ teaspoon cinnamon
¼ teaspoon vanilla
1 teaspoon cornstarch
½ teaspoon grated lemon rind

In top pan of chafing dish over medium flame, combine all ingredients except rind; bring to a boil. Reduce flame to low and simmer sauce 5 minutes, stirring often. Stir in rind and spoon over ice cream.

DESSERT CREPES AND PANCAKES

Henri Charpentier, who served me my first Crêpes Suzette, always maintained that he invented the dish early in the century for the Prince of Wales, later Edward VII, at the Café de la Paris in Monte Carlo, and that when the kirsch accidentally caught fire he covered up by announcing it was a new way of preparing pancakes.

How did his crêpes get the name of Suzette? Why, that was the name of the girl in the prince's party.

CREPES SUZETTE
[Serves 4]

Crêpe batter

3 whole eggs
1 cup flour
4 tablespoons melted butter
1 teaspoon vanilla
1/8 teaspoon grated orange rind

1/2 teaspoon lemon rind
2 tablespoons sugar
Pinch salt
1 cup milk
Butter

Break eggs into mixing bowl. Add flour, butter, vanilla, orange and lemon rind, sugar, salt, and mix well. Beat for 2 or 3 minutes. Add milk. Mix well. Strain through fine sieve.

Fry over low heat in lightly buttered blazer pan, about 7 inches in diameter, using just enough batter for one crêpe to cover the bottom of the pan, and to make 12 crêpes in all. Cook carefully on slow fire, turn and brown evenly on both sides. Stack the 12 crêpes with waxed paper between and keep warm.

Sauce

8 ounces sweet butter	Rind of 4 lemons
8 lumps sugar	4 ponies Cointreau
4 oranges, in halves	4 ponies Curaçao
	4 ounces brandy

As chafing dish warms, melt butter. Rub 4 lumps of sugar against orange rinds and the other 4 against the lemon rinds until they acquire the color of the fruit. Then add the sugar to the melted butter along with the juice of the oranges, squeezed out with the aid of a fork. Stir the mixture gently until sugar is dissolved and the liquid is blended and cooking. Then pour in the Cointreau and Curaçao while the sauce cooks down to ⅔rds and becomes syrupy. This takes approximately 15 minutes. Keep sauce warm in covered bowl.

Next bring in the crêpes from the kitchen and gently fold each twice (into quarter circles) with a fork and spoon. Return ¼ of the sauce to the chafing dish pan and bring to a boil. Place 3 crêpes at a time in the boiling sauce, cover chafing dish and cook for 3 or 4 minutes. Remove the cover and pour 1 ounce of brandy over all and light it. While the fire is blazing, stir the sauce gently with a long-handled spoon. Transfer the crêpes to a hot serving plate and spoon the still-flaming sauce over them.

Repeat with 3 other servings, using ¼ of the sauce and 1 ounce of brandy each time. Crêpes Suzette are eaten with a fork.

ANOTHER LEGENDARY ORIGIN OF CREPES SUZETTE

The Mademoiselle Suzette immortalized in these crêpes was an actress of the Comédie Française at the turn of the last century, who in the 1890's was taking the part of a maidservant required at one moment in the play to serve pancakes.

These were supplied every night from the adjoining Restaurant Marivaux, whose proprietor, the Monsieur Joseph who was afterwards manager of the Savoy Restaurant in London, conceived the idea of igniting them with a glass of brandy so that the audience could assure themselves that the pancakes were genuine.

Sir Harry Luke, in *The Tenth Muse*

"Crêpes Suzette are for one or at most two and if you attempt quantity production with them, you are sunk and wish you hadn't."—James M. Cain.

There's a good deal of truth to the above declaration, so here is a different crêpe recipe for about six people which can be doubled and still made without any trouble.

FLAMING CREPE PIE
[Serves 6]

Crêpes

1 cup flour
4 eggs
2 tablespoons soft butter
1 tablespoon sugar

Grated peel of 1 orange
Grated peel of 1 lemon
Pinch salt
1 cup light cream
Butter

Filling

1 12-ounce jar bitter orange marmalade, berry preserves or plum jam
1 tablespoon sugar

2½ tablespoons water
3 jiggers (4½ ounces) brandy, cognac or applejack

3 lumps sugar

Make batter by combining flour, eggs, butter, sugar, orange and lemon rind and salt and beating well, gradually adding the cream.

Melt a little butter to grease bottom of 6- or 8-inch blazer pan; pour 2 or 3 tablespoons batter into pan—enough to cover bottom—and twist back and forth to spread evenly. Brown crêpe on one side, turn and brown other. When finished, stack on warm plate in warm oven. Repeat until batter is gone.

Place preserves or jam in small saucepan with 1 tablespoon sugar and the water, blend well and bring to a boil. Stir in 1 of the jiggers of brandy and blend again.

Wipe out chafing dish and stack warm crêpes in pan, spreading each with a coating of preserves mixture. Pour remaining mixture over all.

Soak sugar lumps in remaining brandy, place lumps on top of crêpes; pour the rest of brandy over and light.

When flames die down, cut in wedges and serve.

Grand Marnier, Curaçao or Cointreau may be combined with brandy and amount increased to taste.

CREPES POUSSE CAFE
[Serves 4]

Crêpe Batter from Crêpes	Yellow Chartreuse
Suzette (see above)	Maraschino liqueur
Curaçao	Crème de Menthe
Cherry Heering	Confectioners' sugar

Make smaller pancakes so that you get 20 out of recipe, keeping them warm until all are cooked. Stack 5 to a serving, brushing each crêpe with a different liqueur. Dust with sugar and serve hot.

CREPES ST. AUGUSTINE
[Makes 16 crêpes]

Crêpes

2 whole eggs	3 tablespoons all-purpose
2 egg yolks	flour
¼ cup milk	¼ teaspoon salt
2 teaspoons grated orange	1 tablespoon salad oil
rind	Butter

Beat together eggs, egg yolks and half of the milk; add remaining ingredients except butter; beat until blended. Cover and refrigerate 15 minutes. Stir in remaining half of milk.

For each crêpe, heat ½ teaspoon butter in blazer pan. Pour 2 tablespoons batter in side of pan, rotate so mixture covers surface in even layer. Cook, turning once, until lightly browned on both sides. Remove to warm plate and repeat. Then spread Orange Sauce on each crêpe with spoon, fold in quarters and serve immediately.

Orange Sauce

4 tablespoons butter
½ cup fine granulated sugar
1 tablespoon Grand Marnier

3 tablespoons undiluted orange juice concentrate

Cream butter; gradually add sugar; cream again until light and fluffy. Blend in orange juice concentrate and Grand Marnier.

ORANGE CREPES
[Serves 6]

Crêpes

3 eggs
3 egg yolks
½ cup milk
½ cup orange juice
2 tablespoons salad oil
1 tablespoon sugar

1 cup unsifted all-purpose flour
¾ teaspoon salt
1 tablespoon grated orange rind

Beat eggs and yolks; add remaining ingredients and beat until smooth. Let stand at room temperature 1 hour or more.

Lightly brush hot 7- or 8-inch skillet with salad oil.

Add 2 tablespoons batter to skillet, turning and tipping it so mixture covers bottom evenly. Batter will set immediately into thin lacy pancake. When it browns, in 15 to 20 seconds, loosen with spatula and flip over. Brown other side in a few seconds and turn pancake out onto oiled or wax paper. Repeat with remaining batter to make 18 crêpes (6 servings of 3 each).

Orange Sauce No. 2

½ cup soft butter
½ cup confectioners' sugar
1 tablespoon grated orange rind
1 cup orange sections

3 tablespoons Grand Marnier, Cointreau or other orange liqueur
⅓ cup orange juice

Cream butter with sugar and rind; gradually blend in liqueur.

Spread about ½ teaspoon over last side of each crêpe browned (this is the less attractive side).

Roll up crêpes with orange mixture inside.

Place remaining mixture with orange juice in blazer or crêpe pan directly over flame and heat until bubbly. Add rolled crêpes and heat, spooning sauce over. Add orange sections and heat 3 minutes more. Serve at once.

SOUTHERN COMFORT FLAMING CAKES
[Makes 6]

3 eggs, well beaten
1 cup milk
⅓ cup water
1 cup flour
½ teaspoon salt

3 tablespoons sugar
¼ teaspoon baking powder
Preserves or jelly to taste
6 jiggers Southern Comfort, warmed

Confectioners' sugar

Mix eggs, milk and water.

Sift flour, salt, sugar and baking powder together. Add to egg-milk mixture. Blend well. Batter should be very thin.

In lightly greased blazer pan, bake cakes, using ½ cup or less of batter for each. Turn with care and, when brown, remove to hot plate. Sprinkle each with sugar, fill with preserves and roll.

Return pancakes one at a time to blazer pan, pour jigger of Southern Comfort over each, light with long match and serve.

A different kind of crêpes flambées is one of the "happy endings" featured at the Restaurant Lasserre in Paris.

CREPES MYLENE
[Serves 4]

2 ounces butter	3 poached pears, in quarters
2 ounces sugar	2 ounces Mirabelle (plum)
Juice of 2 oranges	brandy [1]
Juice of 1 lemon	2 tablespoons slivered
12 thin medium-sized crêpes	roasted almonds
1 ounce cognac	

Prepare following sauce in blazer pan, over low heat: melt the butter until it is black, mix in the sugar until it dissolves, add the orange and lemon juice along with the cognac.

Prepare 12 crêpes by recipe for Crêpes Suzette Batter above.

Place a quarter of pear in each crêpe, roll up and place rolled crêpes carefully in sauce in pan. Spoon sauce over the crêpes, and drench.

Add Mirabelle brandy, cook for 2 minutes, flaming the crêpes by tipping the pan (or using a match if the heat source is electric). Keep moving the pan back and forth while flaming. Sprinkle with the almonds and serve on warmed plates.

---

[1] Mirabelle brandy is made from yellow plums and comes from Alsace. A substitution can be made with Slivovitz, plum brandy from Hungary.

Here is a variety of dessert pancake served in the Scandinavian countries.

NORTHERN LIGHTS
[Serves 6]

3 cups sifted all-purpose flour	1 quart milk
2 ounces sugar	5 eggs, slightly beaten
2½ teaspoons baking powder	½ cup butter, melted
1 teaspoon salt	Butter for frying
	Berry jam

Whipped cream

Sift together flour, sugar, baking powder and salt; mix well. Gradually stir in milk; add eggs; whip. Add melted butter until mixture is well blended.

Heat blazer pan fairly hot, melt pat of butter in it, remove pan from heat. Pour ½ cup of batter in pan and quickly turn it in all directions so that batter covers bottom. Put back on heat to cook a moment; with cake turner loosen pancake from pan, turn it over and bake other side. Remove to heated plate. Repeat until batter is all used and 24 cakes are made (4 pancakes per serving). Make pancakes as thin as possible, using more milk if batter is too thick.

Place spoonful of jam (in Europe they use lingonberry jam) on each cake, along with spoonful of whipped cream. Fold in four and serve.

Lindy's restaurant on Broadway is gone, but not the memory of the heavenly dessert pancakes they served.

LINDY'S APPLE PANCAKE
[Serves 2]

2 or 3 tablespoons German Pancake Batter (see below)	2 or 3 ripe apples
	2 tablespoons butter
	Cinnamon and sugar, mixed

Make batter as directed in recipe below, using about ⅓ of recipe.

Peel, core and slice the apples thin.

Melt enough butter in large blazer pan to coat bottom and sides; pour very thin coating of batter—2 or 3 table-spoons—in pan, tilt in all directions to spread and bake until brown underneath. Turn with wide spatula, brown other side while covering first browned side with apple slices. Sprinkle cinnamon-sugar mixture over generously, letting heat melt sugar. Remove and serve at once with more cinnamon and sugar on side, cutting pancake in half.

GERMAN PANCAKE BATTER
[Makes about 8 or 10 large cakes]

3 eggs	1/8 teaspoon salt
3/4 cup flour, sifted	1 1/2 teaspoons sugar
	1/2 pint milk

Beat eggs lightly; beat in flour, salt and sugar; then milk. Beat 4 minutes altogether. Batter should be thin and smooth.

LUCHOW'S APPLE PANCAKE
[Serves 2]

Make in the same way as Lindy's Apple Pancake (above) until pancake is covered with apples. Then pour 2 to 3 tablespoons of batter over apples and, when browned on bottom, turn pancake over with wide turner and brown other side.

Fold over like omelet or roll loosely. Cut in half, sprinkle with cinnamon-sugar mixture and serve.

Whole cranberry sauce, blueberry preserves or hot chocolate sauce may be served over or on the side.

From my old friend and operetta collaborator, Robert Stolz, came this Viennese dessert.

COFFEE PANCAKES WITH COFFEE SAUCE
[Serves 6 to 8]

Pancakes

4 ounces flour	½ cup cream
Pinch salt	Butter
1 egg, beaten	Confectioners' sugar
½ cup strong black coffee	Whipped cream

Mix flour, salt, egg and coffee into batter; beat well; then gradually add cream to make thick-pouring consistency.

Fry pancakes in lightly buttered blazer pan; roll each up; sprinkle with sugar and top with whipped cream. Serve with Coffee Sauce on side.

Coffee Sauce

3 tablespoons confectioners' sugar	3 tablespoons cream
1 tablespoon cornstarch	½ cup boiling black coffee
1 tablespoon cocoa	½ cup half-and-half, or light cream

Combine sugar, cornstarch and cocoa in pan; place over medium heat; add cream and stir until thickened; add boiling coffee; stir until completely blended; slowly add half-and-half over heat, but do not boil again. Serve hot.

FRENCH PANCAKE BATTER
[Makes about 2 dozen]

3 eggs	1⅛ cups sifted flour
⅛ teaspoon salt	2 tablespoons salad oil
1½ cups milk	Butter

Beat eggs with salt and milk.

Sift flour again into bowl and add egg mixture, stirring until smooth. Mix in the oil, blend well. Chill 1 hour.

Batter should be consistency of thick cream. If not,

ELECTRIC CHAFING DISH DESSERTS

BASIC CREPES
[Makes 16 6-inch crêpes]

½ cup milk
½ cup water
2 eggs
¼ cup butter or margarine

1 tablespoon sugar
1 tablespoon orange liqueur
1 cup flour
¼ teaspoon salt

Put all ingredients into electric blender container, cover and process at high until smooth. Cover and refrigerate about 2 hours. Lightly grease a 5- or 6-inch blazer or crêpe pan. Heat to sizzling hot. Pour about 3 tablespoons batter into the pan. (A ¼ cup measure is a good ladle.) Immediately tilt pan to completely cover bottom with batter. Cook until golden; crêpes should have a lacy appearance. Turn and cook until golden.

If made in advance, cool crêpes and stack between layers of wax paper. Wrap in foil and refrigerate. To prepare crêpes for serving, let stand at room temperature before folding into fourths to form triangles. Finish with Orange Sauce below.

ORANGE SAUCE FOR CREPES SUZETTE
[Serves 6 or 8]

½ cup butter
½ cup orange juice
Thin rind of 1 orange

¼ cup sugar
¼ cup orange liqueur
16 crêpes from above recipe
⅓ cup cognac or brandy

Melt butter in blazer pan of electric chafing dish at high.

Put orange juice, rind and sugar into blender container, cover and process at high until rind is finely grated.

Pour into blazer pan, stir in orange liqueur. Add crêpes, folded into triangles. Heat to bubbly.

Heat cognac in small sauce pan, pour over crêpes and ignite.

LEMON SOUFFLE CREPES IN ORANGE SAUCE
[Serves 6 to 8]

3 tablespoons butter or margarine	¼ cup sugar
3 tablespoons flour	2 tablespoons lemon juice
⅓ cup milk	2 ½ × 2-inch strips of thin lemon peel
2 eggs, separated	16 cooked crêpes

Put all ingredients except egg whites, 3 tablespoons sugar, and crêpes into blender container, cover and process at high until rind is finely grated.

Pour into small saucepan and cook over low heat, stirring constantly until thickened. Cool while preparing meringue mixture.

Beat egg whites, gradually adding 3 tablespoons sugar until stiff peaks form. Fold in egg yolk mixture.

Spread about 1 tablespoon of filling in center of each crêpe; fold into triangles. Serve with Orange Sauce for Crêpes Suzette.

PINEAPPLE CREAM CREPES IN RUM SAUCE
[Serves 6 to 8]

1 13¼-ounce can crushed pineapple	½ cup confectioners' sugar
1 8-ounce package cream cheese	16 crêpes (see Basic Crêpes recipe)

Drain pineapple, reserving syrup for rum sauce. Combine fruit, cheese and sugar. Refrigerate until ready to use. Place 1 tablespoon of filling in center of each crêpe. Fold in quarters to form a triangle.

Serve with Rum Sauce (see below).

RUM SAUCE
[Serves 6 to 8]

½ cup butter
½ cup brown sugar

½ cup syrup reserved from
    pineapple, or ½ cup
    orange juice
½ cup light rum

Put all ingredients except rum into blazer pan of electric chafing dish. Cook uncovered at high until slightly thickened, about 7 minutes.

Arrange folded crêpes in four layers in blazer pan. Heat to bubbly.

Heat rum in small saucepan. Pour over crêpes and ignite.

FLAMING PEACH SUNDAE
[Serves 4 to 6]

1 1-pound, 13-ounce can
    sliced peaches, with syrup
¼ cup brown sugar
1 tablespoon cornstarch

2 tablespoons butter
⅓ cup brandy flavored with
    ½ teaspoon powdered
    ginger

Ice cream

Drain syrup from peaches. Reserve syrup, and mix ½ cup with sugar and cornstarch until smooth.

Heat remaining syrup in blazer pan of electric chafing dish at high. Add sugar mixture and cook, stirring constantly until thickened. Add butter and peaches. Heat through. Place over hot water bath and keep warm at medium setting.

To serve, heat brandy in small saucepan, pour over peaches and ignite. Spoon over servings of ice cream.

Variations:

Apricots with apricot brandy.

Pineapple with light rum or orange-flavored liqueur.

Strawberries or raspberries with kirsch or orange-flavored liqueur.

With these fruits use white instead of brown sugar.

Flaming Coffee Drinks
and Other Beverages

As served at the Caribbean Room of the Pontchartrain Hotel in New Orleans, Café Brûlot is always a flaming success. You, too, can dish out this coffee spectacular right from your home chafing dish, either as the happy ending of a satisfying dinner, or after an evening of conversation . . . or even following the Late, Late Show.

ORANGE CAFE BRULOT
[Serves 5 to 6]

2-inch stick cinnamon
Peel of 1 orange
Peel of 1 lemon
12 cloves

1 ounce Grand Marnier
2 ounces orange Curaçao
2 ounces brandy
1 pint very strong coffee

Break cinnamon stick into pieces in deep chafing dish.

Peel orange and lemon in continuous spirals. Insert cloves into orange peel. Add peels to chafing dish.

Ignite Sterno under dish. Pour in Grand Marnier, Curaçao and brandy and keep mixing and crushing peels and cinnamon as mixture comes to boil.

Flame by lighting hot contents with taper or long match; agitate with ladle or long silver spoon. Very slowly add coffee, stirring constantly. When flame dies, serve in brûlot or demitasse cups.

CAFE DIABLE
[Serves 4 to 6]

3 small cubes sugar
¼ cup butter or margarine
1 cup whole roasted coffee
  beans
Grated rind of 1 orange
Chopped peel of 1 apple
2-inch stick cinnamon

12 cloves
6 tablespoons cognac or
  brandy
6 tablespoons kirsch
6 tablespoons Curaçao
1¼ cups fresh-made coffee
Juice of 1 orange

Put sugar and butter in chafing dish or diable pan over direct flame. Melt butter but do not brown. Add coffee beans, orange and apple peel, cinnamon and cloves. Pour in cognac, kirsch and Curaçao; stir and heat. Flame, preferably by tipping pan so liqueur fumes are ignited by Sterno flame. When flame dies out, add coffee and orange juice; heat to steaming. Pour through strainer into demitasse cups.

RUM-LACED COFFEE
[Serves 6]

1 quart very strong coffee
1 teaspoon whole cloves
2 sticks cinnamon

12 lumps sugar
Grated rind of 1 orange
¼ cup brandy

½ cup light rum, warmed

Pour coffee into top pan of chafing dish. Add cloves, cinnamon sticks, sugar and grated orange rind. Heat thoroughly and add brandy.

Pour a little warmed rum into a metal ladle and ignite it over chafing dish; spoon the coffee up and over. Continue adding rum, burn for a moment before dipping into the chafing dish and ladling again. When rum and flame are gone, serve.

COFFEE AU RHUM
[Serves 6 or 7]

6 cups very strong coffee
6 lumps sugar
1 lemon

6 whole cloves
1 stick cinnamon
1 cup light rum

Prepare coffee and keep hot.

Rub sugar on the rind of lemon. Place sugar in top pan of chafing dish over direct medium flame with cloves, cinnamon stick and thinly sliced rind from half of the lemon. Add warmed rum, bring just to a boil, stirring until sugar is dissolved. Do not let it catch fire. Add coffee and bring to boil again. Serve at once.

IRISH COFFEE
[Serves 4 to 6]

3 cups fresh-made strong coffee

4 ounces Irish whisky
Semi-stiff whipping cream

Pour coffee into chafing dish or diable pan over direct flame. Add 2 ounces of the whisky.

Heat remaining 2 ounces of whisky in ladle. Ignite and pour over coffee mixture and stir until flame dies away. Serve in Irish coffee glasses and float the cream on top, pouring it over a teaspoon held upside down near coffee.

CAFE OLE
[Serves 4 to 6]

3 cups fresh-made coffee
1/4 teaspoon grated lemon rind
1/4 cup (2 ounces) coffee
    liqueur

1/2 cup Irish whisky
Whipped cream

Pour coffee and lemon rind into chafing dish or diable pan over direct flame. Add coffee liqueur and 1/4 cup of the whisky. Heat remaining 1/4 cup whisky in ladle; ignite; pour over coffee mixture and stir until flame dies. Serve in Irish coffee glasses, topped with whipped cream.

ELECTRIC CHAFING DISH BEVERAGES

HOT CHOCOLATE
[Makes 1 quart]

3 squares unsweetened
    chocolate
½ cup hot water
½ cup sugar

1 2-inch stick cinnamon
Dash salt
3½ cups hot milk
Marshmallows

Put chocolate in blazer pan of electric chafing dish over hot water bath at high. Stir occasionally until melted. Add water, sugar, cinnamon and salt and cook at medium setting, stirring occasionally, until smooth and slightly thickened. Stir in milk.

Remove cinnamon and serve with marshmallows on top.

Variation: As a special adult treat, lace with ¼ to ½ cup sherry.

HOT RUMMED CIDER
[Serves 6 to 8]

1½ quarts apple cider
  6 tablespoons brown sugar

3 tablespoons butter
1½ cups light rum

Bring cider and sugar to boiling in blazer pan of electric chafing dish at high. Place over hot water bath at medium setting. Add butter. When melted, add rum.

CAFE BRULOT DIABLE
[Serves 8 to 10]

1½ cups cognac
¼ cup sugar
12 whole cloves

1 2-inch cinnamon stick
Thin rind of 1 lemon
Thin rind of 1 orange

3 cups strong hot coffee

Place cognac, sugar, cloves, cinnamon and lemon and orange rinds into blazer pan of electric chafing dish over hot water bath at high. Stir occasionally until cognac is heated through. Light the cognac and continue to stir with long-handled silver spoon while it burns. After a minute or two slowly pour in the coffee while stirring. When the flame subsides, ladle into heated demitasses, being careful not to serve the spices or rinds.

SMUGGLER'S BREW
[Serves 8]

1½ cups dark rum
1 quart tea
3 tablespoons butter
½ cup sugar

Thin rind of ½ lemon
½ teaspoon nutmeg
Lemon slices
½ cup brandy

Heat all ingredients, except brandy and lemon slices, to boiling in blazer pan of electric chafing dish at high. Place over hot water bath at medium setting. Garnish with lemon slices. Heat brandy in small saucepan and add to rum mixture. Flame and serve in demitasses.

Catalog of Chafing Dish Equipment[1]

BLOOMINGDALE'S DEPARTMENT STORES: Large selection of c.d.s from various countries at various prices.

BONGUSTO: (Italian) Copperware with tin lining and brass fittings, large capacity, $60, Gimbels.

CIRCA 21 by VOLLRATH: (U.S.) Stainless steel set consisting of 2-quart covered saucepan/fondue dish, 1½-quart casserole–double boiler inset, over Flambeau table server, $43.85, The Pot Rack at A. L. Cahn & Sons, Inc., Park Avenue, N.Y.C.

DOURO: (Portuguese) Solid copperware, tin-lined and brass, $20, Macy's.

FORTUNOFF STORES: New York and Long Island, 2-quart, stainless steel, Sterno burner, walnut finish handle, legs and knob, $10.98 on sale.

GIMBELS DEPARTMENT STORES: Large, copper, $24.99; Copper and aluminum-lined, $23; Stainless steel, $19.95.

JAPANESE: Medium copper and brass, $25; Small, copper and stainless steel, $16.99, Macy's.

KORVETTE STORES: 4-quart pewtertone, Mediterranean motif, alcohol burner, $12.99 on sale. Stainless steel set, $17.99; (Taiwan) Enamel, $7.99; (Italian) Spun steel, $19.95. Oster Electric, $29.99. Cornwall Electric, $19.99.

MACY'S DEPARTMENT STORES: (Carrier Shop) Double copper, $50; (Basement store) (Japanese) yellow enamel, $22.99; (Japanese) enamel exterior, $19.99, also stainless steel, $19.99; (Japanese) Large stainless steel, $14.95.

---

[1] Where prices are quoted, they are the ones prevalent in New York City in the Spring of 1971.

OSTER: Electric chafing dish with controlled heat, 2½-quart blazer pan Teflon II lined; in Avocado, Harvest Gold or Flame, also polished aluminum.

RONSON: Varaflame Table Chef, a portable butane gas range. No smoke, odor, spill or spatter. Control on handle. Comes in standard stand ($26.95), deluxe stand ($32.50), and double burner ($49.50), also Cook-ette with 6-point flame ($13.50). Can be used as heat source for chafing dish (not provided). Butane lasts 4 to 10 hours, refills, $1.49.

SPRING: (Swiss) Eight different alcohol flamers, 5 pans and Buffet-Butler chafing dish of Culinox, also in stainless steel; 2½-quart, copper, stainless-steel lined, $40, The Pot Rack at A. L. Cahn & Sons, Inc., Park Avenue, N.Y.C., and The Pampered Kitchen, Greenwich Village, N.Y.C.

TAGUS: (Portuguese) Single enamel blazer pan, $17.99, Macy's.

VOLLRATH: (U.S.) Stainless steel, Deluxe Chafer with "slide-out" burner, includes wood-handled rack, 4-inch water pan, 2½-inch inset pan and lucite dome cover, $80; Economy Chafer with "slide-out" burner, includes wire rack, 4-inch water pan, 2½-inch inset pan and lucite dome cover, $60, both at A. L. Cahn & Sons, Inc., N.Y.C.

WIDE WORLD IMPORT BAZAAR: Pasadena, North Hollywood and Beverly Hills, Calif. Wide assortment of popular-priced (mainly Japanese) chafing dish sets and accessories (author's brother heads this chain).

CHAFING DISH FUELS, SOLID

STERNO CANNED HEAT COOKING FUEL, in 2½-ounce (29¢) and 7-ounce (59¢) cans. Since 1887.

CHAFING DISH FUELS, LIQUID

STERNO CHAFING DISH LIQUID FUEL, Sterno, Inc., New York 10022; for liquid alcohol burning units; nontoxic, smokeless, lemon-scented, flip-top spout, plastic container; flammable, keep away from eyes and children, 12 ounces, $1.39.

MORE ABOUT CHAFING DISH EQUIPMENT

If you do not have a chafing dish set and are chafing to try some of the c.d. recipes, you can begin with a pan or skillet and a source of heat such as a can of Sterno on a stand of some sort. This is possible because the skillet-like blazer pan is the principal utensil used in chafing dish cookery.

The water pan or *bain-marie* acts as the bottom of a double boiler, modifying the heat and keeping food warm. And, if you have a recipe which calls for steaming, you need a cover for the pan. But with the regulation chafing dish set, when the water pan is used, it is filled about 1/3 full of hot or boiling water.

Chafing dishes are made of many materials: copper with tin or aluminum or stainless steel lining; aluminum or stainless steel throughout; enamel over cast iron; pewter; even sterling silver.

The sizes go all the way from small, for sauces and desserts, to big ones for 8 people; for soup and for main dishes. And there are other pans beside the conventional blazer—omelet pans, crêpe pans, buffet or saucepans and Dutch pans with the largest capacity.

AND BURNERS

Most popular sources of heat are canned, which means Sterno, and alcohol burners, either with a wick or a fiberglass pad. The alcohol is the wood or denatured kind, bought in hardware or drug stores, and is very poisonous if drunk. Keep the bottle or tin where it cannot be accidentally used for any other purpose but fuel. Fill burner away from table or any wood surface, which alcohol would ruin, and be sure the outside is dry before using. Fill only 1/2 full and *never* when either aflame or still hot.

Wick-type burners are regulated by raising or lowering the wick; the others by opening or closing the damper; Sterno, by sliding the lid. To avoid possibility of fire, alcohol burners should be either covered tightly or emptied of fuel when storing chafing dish.

Electric and butane heat sources should be operated and cleaned according to the instruction of the manufacturers.

Candlepower is so weak that this type of warmer is not used, except possibly to keep dessert sauces warm.

Index